Spiritual Warfare According to Grace

THE FLESH

Preston Condra | Kelly Condra

sufficient✝word
MINISTRIES

www.sufficientword.com

Spiritual Warfare According to Grace
The Flesh
Preston Condra and Kelly Condra

Sufficient Word Publishing, a division of Sufficient
Word Ministries, Inc., Springdale, AR.
Copyright © 2023 Preston Condra and Kelly Condra
Printed in the United States of America. All rights reserved.

Unless otherwise indicated, all Scripture quotations are taken from
the KING JAMES VERSION of the Bible, public domain.

Scripture quotations marked (NASB) are taken from the New American
Standard Bible®. Copyright ©1960, 1962, 1963, 1968, 1971, 1972, 1973,
1975, 1977, 1995 by The Lockman Foundation. Used by permission.

Scripture quotations marked (NKJV) have been taken from the
Holy Bible, NEW KING JAMES VERSION®, Copyright © 1982 by
Thomas Nelson, Inc. Used by permission. All rights reserved.

Bolded text was added to some verses for emphasis.

Production and design by Sufficient Word Ministries
and Madison Lux: *upwork.com/fl/madisonlux*
Cover artwork by Emma Hall.

ISBN: 978-1-946245-55-7

It was for freedom that Christ set us free; therefore keep standing firm and do not be subject again to a yoke of slavery. (Gal 5:1 NASB)

Contents

Preface. ix

Introduction: The Elements of Victory 1

Chapter 1: Three Types of Men, Three Parts of Man 9

Chapter 2: The Swamp of the Flesh 19

Romans 8:1-13 31

Chapter 3: The Law of Sin in the Flesh 33

Romans 7:1-11 45

Chapter 4: Understanding the Nature of Law:
Romans 7:1-11 47

Romans 7:12-25 55

Chapter 5: Understanding the Conflict: Romans 7:12-25. . . . 57

Chapter 6: Imputation, Baptism, and the New Covenant. . . 67

Romans 6:1-12 75

Chapter 7: Reckoning in Practice: Romans 6:1-12 77

Romans 6:13-23 85

Chapter 8: Know, Reckon, Yield: Romans 6:13-23. 87

Conclusion: He Did it All 97

Preface

If a Christian was asked how many spiritual enemies he had, he might know that he had three: the world, the flesh, and the devil. If he was asked about spiritual warfare, he might mention the armor of God which is found in Ephesians Chapter Six. That chapter describes the method of victory against "the wiles of the devil," but makes no mention of the other two enemies. We, the authors, suspect that many Christians have prayed through the armor of God only to find that their battle with temptation has not ceased. What a discouragement to go to God's word with the intention to obey, and yet find no victory there! The problem, certainly, is not with God's word or the armor; it is due to the fact that armor does not help when the enemy is inside the armor. A Christian must first learn to have victory within before he can consistently walk free from the enemies that attack him from without. To live in spiritual freedom is to recognize and defeat:

- The temptation to succumb to the sinful nature of the flesh.
- Satanic deception regarding the teachings of God's word.
- The distractions of the world—including "good" things— which fill the believer's life, keeping him from fulfilling God's will as revealed in the epistles to the church.

As we, the authors, contemplated a project on spiritual warfare, it quickly became apparent that the teachings regarding our enemies could fill many books. Because the enemy within—the flesh—is the first hurdle in spiritual freedom, we decided that the devil and his world system will have to wait for a later book. This book, therefore, focuses on freedom from what Paul calls "the law of sin" and its most deceptive trigger—the Law itself, the Law of Moses.

We believe that information about spiritual warfare is necessary for believers as soon as they are saved. A new Christian soon comes under attack, and successive defeats early in his Christian life can lead to discouragement and disillusionment from which he may never recover. He must learn that he has tools with which he can free himself.

> *Forasmuch then as Christ hath suffered for us in the flesh, **arm yourselves** likewise with the same mind:* (1 Pet 4:1a)

> *Likewise reckon ye also **yourselves** to be dead indeed unto sin, but alive unto God through Jesus Christ our Lord.* (Ro 6:11)

> *For the grace of God that bringeth salvation hath appeared to all men, Teaching us that, **denying** ungodliness and worldly lusts, we should live soberly, righteously, and godly, in this present world;* (Titus 2:11-12)

> *Examine **yourselves**, whether ye be* (operating) *in the faith; prove your own selves. Know ye not your own selves, how that Jesus Christ is in you, except ye be reprobates?* (2 Cor 13:5, clarification added)

> *And that they may **recover themselves** out of the snare of the devil, who are taken captive by him at his will.* (2 Tim 2:26)

The Christian's three enemies were defeated on the cross; no saint need live under their dominion. Nonetheless, every Christian on earth still lives in a sin-cursed body and in a fallen world.

Therefore, each must exercise faith in those promises of God which teach him that he has been made free.

Every new circumstance in life can lead to new temptations; no Christian is ever "done" in regard to spiritual warfare. Learning to recognize and defeat one's spiritual enemies in both old and new situations is vital to triumph in Christ. Our triumph—by His power—glorifies Him, encourages other Christians, and enables us to do God's will. We pray this book will bless its readers in its attempt to explain the enemy, the battle, and the glorious victory available in Christ by God's marvelous grace.

> *For all things* are *for your sakes, that the abundant grace might through the thanksgiving of many redound to the glory of God. For which cause we faint not; but though our outward man perish, yet the inward* man *is renewed day by day. For our light affliction, which is but for a moment, worketh for us a far more exceeding* and *eternal weight of glory;* (2 Cor 4:15-17)

> *Now thanks* be *unto God, which always causeth us to triumph in Christ, and maketh manifest the savour of his knowledge by us in every place.* (2 Cor 2:14)

Introduction
The Elements of Victory

Victory over the flesh could be summarized in one word: RECKON. Romans Chapter Six, the manual on defeating the flesh, is all about what a Christian is to reckon, meaning to count to be true. The saint who understands what Christ accomplished, and believes God in regard to the always-available victory, can swiftly put away temptation and be Christlike, regardless of his circumstances. He reckons (counts) to be true what God says is true. What does God say is true? That we have been made free. Our freedom from all three spiritual enemies has already been accomplished. Spiritual victory is a matter of knowing and using what we have in Christ.

But I Don't Have a Problem

Doubtless there are some who imagine that spiritual warfare looks like a scene from a horror movie, replete with screaming girls and spinning heads. Such a person might think, "I haven't killed anyone, cheated on my spouse, or beat my kids. I don't think this spiritual warfare stuff applies to me." Perhaps it is true that I am not as bad as I could be, but I must consider this: Am I as holy as God? Because that is what He has called us to be:

But as he which hath called you is holy, so be ye holy in all manner of conversation; Because it is written, Be ye holy; for I am holy. (1 Pet 1:15-16; see also Lev 20:7)

If I am not sure that I am spiritually free from the influence of my flesh and living according to God's will, I could ask myself questions like these: Do I have "the patience of a saint" in traffic? Do I walk through most days filled with joy and thankfulness to God? Do I desire the pure gold of God's word more than anything? Do I share the Gospel whenever possible? Would others describe me as completely sold out to Jesus to the exclusion of nearly every other earthly pursuit? No one alive can say, "Yes," to such things all the time, but a maturing Christian will find that such things increasingly characterize his life. His yieldedness to Christ's work in him is more consistent, more visible, and more enjoyable as he goes through life.

Already Free

...where the Spirit of the Lord is, there is liberty. (2 Cor 3:17b)

Regardless of which enemy is attacking, the fact is that every Christian has already been made able to defeat it. From the moment we believe the Gospel, 1 Corinthians 15:1-4, we are *already* free not to sin, because salvation has ongoing benefits. After initial salvation, the Gospel of Christ continues to save us from sin, by faith. That truth could be the end of this book; when tempted to sin, believe that you do not have to sin and don't; end of story! And yet, much of the content of the letters to the Church address sinning, deceived Christians who are not using what they have in Christ. So why does there seem to be a disconnection between what the Bible says about us and how we actually live?

There are several reasons for the gap which Christians often see in themselves and in others when comparing their observations to how the Bible describes Christian living. If a Christian does not know what God has promised him, if he cannot recognize an enemy attack or does not know what weapons he has at his disposal, a difference between scriptural words and earthly experience will exist. The saint who studies to gain a deeper knowledge of God's word and applies what he learns will see the scripture/experience gap diminish. By faith in the promises of God, a Christian can be Christ-like in his motives, attitude, actions, and words. Normal Christian living should feel peaceful, calm, stable, drama-free, anxiety free, and wholesome. It is meant to be filled with love and kindness, patience and forgiveness, and biblical wisdom and knowledge. The lack of these qualities indicates the influence of a spiritual enemy.

Spiritual Toolbox

For victory, the first enemy that must be mastered is the one on the inside—the flesh. Operating in the flesh is most often just "being yourself," rather than being Christlike. Galatians 5:22-23 lists several aspects of Christlikeness, also known as spirituality, and is followed by this statement:

> *And they that are Christ's have crucified the flesh with the affections and lusts.* (Gal 5:24)

The previous verse tells us that the flesh must be effectively "dead" in regard to Christian living. This rules out "being yourself" as a norm for Christian life; it requires that we use the weapons (instruments, tools) provided by God to render the flesh powerless. One's fleshly nature can range from generic "blah" to self-righteous piety to the foulest moral degradation and everything in between, but all fleshly sin is dealt with using the same tool—reckoning; that is not, however, the weapon used against Satan. Consider the fact that many occupations have tools particular to their work. So too, Christians have tools that belong to our position in Christ so that we might do ours. These tools (weapons) enable us to operate in a way that is worthy of the exalted position that we have been given.

The Christian's primary tool is knowledge: Christianity is a relationship with God based on knowing. God put in writing those things which He wants us to know. Eternal life itself is defined as knowing Him (Jhn 17:3). All of Christian living is accomplished by God's grace through faith; so too is spiritual warfare. But victory is inestimably more attainable when a Christian thoroughly understands the "what" and the "how" of spiritual warfare under grace. The victorious saint must:

- Know the character of his own flesh so as to recognize an attack.
- Understand the operation of the law of sin so as to understand the battle that is happening inside himself.
- Know the solution: to reckon to be true those things that are true of Christ, which were granted to us in spiritual baptism.

The Necessity of Using the Tools Given to the *Church*

A Christian who learns to be spiritual and lives accordingly will rapidly become the object of spiritual attack. A Christian's understanding of and faith in grace principles appropriates the powerful spiritual blessings that were won for him on the cross. These blessings are not found outside the teachings (doctrines) of grace; they are the spiritual blessings to the Church which were kept secret until after the resurrection of Christ (1 Cor 2:7-8, Ro 16:25). Only the doctrines of the Church can defeat the enemies of its members.

We, the authors, decided to write a book about spiritual warfare *according to grace* in order to help Christians arm themselves for the realities of spiritual life. Many "spiritual warfare" materials attempt to access the authority and miraculous powers of Jesus Christ and the Apostles from the first century period of signs and wonders. This will not work. Although we believe that Satan does sometimes cease an attack when such attempts are made, it would only be for the greater victory of keeping people deceived. Ultimately, there will be no long-term solution nor spiritual fruit from attempting to reproduce miracles which were intended to prove to the Jewish nation that their earthly, Davidic kingdom was at hand.

> *These twelve Jesus sent forth, and commanded them, saying, Go not into the way of the Gentiles, and into* any *city of the Samaritans enter ye not: But go rather to the lost sheep of the house of Israel. And as ye go, preach, saying, The kingdom of heaven is at hand. Heal the sick, cleanse the lepers, raise the dead, cast out devils…* (Mat 10:5-8a)

Those who had the authority to cast out demons were also able to heal on demand with a 100% success rate, raise the dead, handle dangerous snakes without risk, drink poison with no effect, and multiply food; this is clearly not the current program. Furthermore, Jesus' miracles were not random selections; feeding, healing, and casting out demons were kingdom signs. They foreshadowed the conditions of that one-thousand-year period when the curse will be rolled back; the kingdom will have no sickness, no hunger, and Satan will be bound in a pit. By avoiding this very important contextual information, some teachers encourage the saints to directly contend with demons as Jesus did. Doing so is absolutely not for the Church. Paul and the other epistle writers never instruct Christians to do so. Rightly dividing the word of truth is imperative for spiritual victory.

> *Study to shew thyself approved unto God, a workman that needeth not to be ashamed, rightly dividing the word of truth.* (2 Tim 2:15)

According to Grace and Only by Faith

The writer of the epistle to the Hebrew Christians repeatedly reminded the saints that what we have in Christ is better than what they left behind in Judaism. The same is true in spiritual warfare. Before the resurrection of Christ, the best that could be done was to cast out a demon who could return. The person was without protection because he was not indwelt by God nor sealed with the Holy Spirit. Christians have no need to cast out demons; we have the Gospel, the power of God unto salvation! When a person hears and believes the message of the cross, he receives immediate deliverance and protection. Furthermore, God does not discriminate between persons for any reason other than their own desire to reject Him. Nowhere does it say that a person who is being disturbed, oppressed, or possessed by demons cannot believe the Gospel. There is no biblical instruction to "deliver" a person in order for them to be saved; adding any such requirement to the Gospel is in itself a denial of its sufficient power unto salvation.

The wiles of the devil are subtle, and the susceptibility of the human mind to deception is enormous. The importance of knowing the truth *according to grace* cannot be overstated. The same is true of operating by faith; the Christian life operates by no other means. No Christian is stuck with, "This is just my personality," "This is how I was raised," "I'll never get over this," or any other reason for believing that consistent spiritual maturity—i.e., Christlikeness—is not possible. Grace is sufficient. A Christian must possess this conviction for spiritual victory (Ja 1:6-7).

Because each of us lives in a body tainted with sin, we will not live in perfect spiritual freedom, but he who is convinced that God's will is better than anything offered by the world, the flesh, or the devil, and endeavors to learn it, can live consistently as a mature, spiritual man, bringing glory to God in daily living. This begins with learning to live free from the swamp of sin known as "the flesh." From his position of triumph in Christ, he can also lead others out of the coming fire.

> *And others save with fear, pulling* them *out of the fire; hating even the garment spotted by the flesh.* (Jude 1:23)

Chapter One

Three Types of Men,
Three Parts of Man

KEY CONCEPTS:

- **God recognizes 3 types of men: natural, spiritual, carnal.**
- **God made us with 3 parts: spirit, soul, body.**
- **To sin is to operate independently from God.**

The payment for the sins of the world was made by Jesus Christ on the cross and was sufficient to satisfy the sin debt of all mankind throughout all of history. Jesus' payment is what delivers from condemnation those who believe the Gospel, 1 Corinthians 15:1-4. The Apostle Paul, who sometimes used the phrase, "my Gospel," received additional revelation regarding the good news of salvation: that the saints had also received a "total package" of salvation benefits. We are not only free from the penalty for sin, but also from its power in daily living, and ultimately from its presence when we go to be with the Lord. Paul taught these spiritual truths personally to the other Apostles (Gal 2:1-2) and to the entire Church through his epistles.

Because of the propitiatory (fully satisfying) sacrifice of Christ on the cross, every person who has believed the Gospel has been saved from sin. Each saint is to learn to live in accordance with the victory over sin which Jesus Christ won. We must be aware of our spiritual benefits and know how to use them.

Three Types of Men: Natural, Spiritual, and Carnal

Using one's spiritual benefit package begins with discerning one's spiritual condition. The saint who can determine his current state can apply the truths of God's word appropriately so as to walk consistently in victory over sin. In God's current administration (which is by grace through faith and not by law), all mankind exists in one of three spiritual conditions:

- Natural
- Spiritual
- Carnal

The first kind of man is the *natural man*. He is natural because he is in the condition in which he was born: dead in trespasses and sins. He is spiritually dead because he is separated from God, the source of spiritual life. He exists always and only in the swamp of his flesh because he has no other means of operation. Even if he seems to be "good," nothing he does pleases God because all that he is and does is tainted with sin (Ro 3:12). The natural man needs deliverance from sin, and only God can deliver him. This deliverance is known as salvation, and it is a result of simply believing the Gospel message of 1 Corinthians 15:1-4.

Faith alone in the death, burial, and resurrection of Christ for the purpose of salvation from sin results in spiritual regeneration, also known as being "born again." In regeneration, the human spirit is joined with God's spirit and is, thereby, given spiritual life. No longer separated from God (i.e., dead) in trespasses and sins, the believer is now indwelt by God and will *never again* be a natural man. His spiritual birth is by faith in the sufficient work of Jesus Christ and has nothing whatsoever to do with his qualities or efforts. He is simply trusting in the work of another. He is safe, having been sealed with the Holy Spirit unto the day of redemption. He is part of Christ's inheritance and will never be lost. He may lose rewards for not living in accordance with his salvation, but once he is born, he is born. (See 2 Cor 1:22; Eph 1:13, 4:30; Jhn 18:9)

The spiritual communion of regeneration provides the believer with a new spiritual condition; he can now live as a *spiritual man*. As such, he is filled with the Spirit of God, emanates God's character, and is immediately empowered to live according to God's will, free from the dominion of sin. The Christian who learns how to be consistently spiritual (Spirit-filled) is able to deny the principle (law) of sin which operates in his body. If he does not learn how to do so, or if he chooses to live independently from God, he becomes a *carnal man*, remaining under the dominion of his sinful nature. To be carnal—also known as fleshly—is the third spiritual condition of man. To be carnal is to live according to the motivations and desires of the flesh. His life might or might not appear to be obviously sinful. The carnal man possesses salvation, but he is not using its benefits for daily living and could be living like any natural man. Some in the church in Corinth were living in this way:

> …*are ye not carnal and walk as* (natural) *men*? (1 Cor 3:3b, clarification added)

The carnal man is using the same operating system as the natural man—the flesh. Regardless of the outward appearance of his life, he is not living by the power of God. He might read the Bible, but he cannot appropriate its benefits. He might do what appears to be good works, but he is not doing them in the correct, Spirit-filled way. Because sin is progressive, if he persists in carnality, he will not do those "good works" for long.

> *I speak after the manner of men because of the infirmity of your flesh: for as ye have yielded your members servants to uncleanness and to **iniquity unto iniquity**; even so now yield your members servants to righteousness unto holiness.* (Ro 6:19)

Because sin dwells in each human body for as long as it lives on this earth, the potential to sin is always present. From moment to moment, every Christian has the choice to cooperate with God or to act independently from Him. Only a spiritual man can please God, because he is operating by faith in God's promises to the church.

> *Because the carnal mind is enmity against God: for it is not subject to the law of God, neither indeed can be.* (Ro 8:7)

If a carnal Christian recognizes his sin, he can use the proper biblical prescription to return to spiritual operation: he can change his mind in regard to the sin (repent) and return to agreement with the applicable scriptural truth (confess). If he matures in his Christian life, he will learn to reckon himself dead to sin *before* he succumbs to temptation, a topic covered in detail in Chapters Seven and Eight of this book. In doing so, he will maintain his spiritual condition and avoid becoming carnal.

The Battle Against Sin is in the Mind

Man's fall into sin happened because of an idea. Eve thought that Eden's forbidden fruit looked appealing, and she was deceived into thinking that the serpent's claim had merit. Adam apparently thought it would be better to go along with Eve's suggestion than to speak against it. The entrance of sin into daily living has not changed. How things look and seem to us apart from God's word can quickly draw us away from spiritual living and back under the dominion of our sinful nature.

The human mind has two parts; one part is the human spirit, which is the "knowing" part of man (1 Cor 2:11). The spirit must be continually reminded of truth in order to combat the onslaught of lies from the flesh, the devil, and the world system (Ro 12:2, 2 Cor 4:16, Eph 4:23, Col 3:10). Adam and Eve began life without these enemies. Adam was created in the image of God, and Eve was built from Adam. Because their bodies were free from the law of sin, they enjoyed fellowship (communion) with God. Because of their fall into sin, every human being since Adam and Eve has been born separated from God by sin. Adam and Eve could not pass on to their children the sinless condition which they no longer had; the descendants that they **generated** were in *their* image.

> *And Adam lived an hundred and thirty years, and begat a son in his own likeness, after his image; and called his name Seth:* (Gen 5:3)

Spiritual fellowship between God and man would not be restored until the penalty for sin had been paid and man's spirit could be **regenerated**, a biblical concept that is also referred to by its various writers as "begotten again," "born of the Spirit," "born of God," or "born again."

Not by works of righteousness which we have done, but
according to his mercy he saved us, by the washing of
regeneration, *and renewing of the Holy Ghost;* (Titus 3:5)

Adam's choice to rebel against God began with an erroneous idea; that led to an unrighteous desire which was offensive to God and resulted in his condemnation. Adam's offense was that his motives and desires changed from loving obedience to self-centered independence. The spirit within him was now of an unrighteous quality, rendering him unfit for fellowship (communion) with God; Adam and Eve were now spiritually dead: separated from the relationship with Him that they had previously enjoyed. The act of sin (disobedience) that followed Adam's offensive intent initiated a new way of operating, making sinners of all mankind. A savior from sin was now needed.

> *Therefore as by the* **offence** *of one judgment came upon all*
> *men to condemnation; even so by the righteousness of one*
> the free gift came *upon all men unto justification of life.*
> *For as by one man's disobedience many were made sinners,*
> *so by the obedience of one shall many be made righteous.*
> (Ro 5:18-19)

All those born in the centuries since the fall of Adam were natural men. They could be nothing else until mankind's sins were paid and God could once again commune with man.

The Three Parts of Man

Understanding spirituality and carnality in the believer is aided by an understanding of his three parts: spirit, soul, and body. The body is the physical part of man; its various parts, such as hands and eyes, are called its members.

… I pray God *your whole spirit and soul and body be preserved blameless unto the coming of our Lord Jesus Christ.* (1 Thes 5:23b)

The difference between the spirit and soul is that the spirit knows, while the soul feels and is also the seat of volition. (Sometimes the word "soul" is translated "heart" to indicate the volitional function of the soul. See Eph 6:6 and Col 3:23.) These three parts are mentioned again by James, whose church members were struggling with carnality.

This wisdom descendeth not from above, but is earthly, sensual, devilish. (Ja 3:15. Note: The word "sensual" is literally the word "soulish," and is sometimes translated "natural," because the natural man operates only according to his own will. See also Jde 1:19; 2 Cor 2:14; 1 Cor 15:44, 46)

Notice that the same three parts of man listed in 1 Thessalonians 5:23 are referred to in reverse order and in a different way than in James 3:15, indicating the source of the influence acting upon them. This is so because carnality operates in the opposite way than does spirituality. **In a spiritual man, the word of God feeds the human spirit, which turns the will of man toward God's will, affecting the operation of his body—in his behavior and words, for example.**

Spiritual Man:
TRUTH → HUMAN SPIRIT →
WILL OF THE SOUL → BODY USED FOR GOD'S WILL

Eve's choice in the garden was not informed by what God said, but by one of her physical senses—what she saw. Her soul, the seat of volition, was swayed by her desire for the fruit, and her spirit was deceived by the devilish temptation. The flow of influence was reversed.

Natural Man/Carnal Man:

TEMPTATION → PHYSICAL SENSES →
WILL OF THE SOUL → HUMAN SPIRIT → SIN

The carnal man's soul is responding to the temptations perceived by his bodily senses; he is carnal because the desires of his soul are influencing his spirit and deceiving him. The spiritual man is not deceived because his spirit is influenced by truth. Therefore, the desire of his soul is to obey God.

> *For they that are after the flesh do mind the things of the flesh; but they that are after the Spirit the things of the Spirit.* (Ro 8:5)

The flesh is always at war against the soul, drawing the human will toward its desires. When the flesh succeeds in seducing the soul (the seat of volition), the believer is carnal. He is captive to sin until he repents, which means he changes his mind in regard to the sin.

> *Dearly beloved, I beseech* you *as strangers and pilgrims, abstain from fleshly lusts, which war against the soul;* (1 Pet 2:11)

> *Knowing this, that our old man is crucified with* him, *that the body of sin might be destroyed, that henceforth we should not serve sin. … Let not sin therefore reign in your mortal body, that ye should obey it in the lusts thereof.* (Ro 6:6, 12)

Having therefore these promises, dearly beloved, let us cleanse ourselves from all filthiness of the flesh and spirit, perfecting holiness in the fear of God. (2 Cor 7:1)

Sin is independence from God

Sin tends to be equated with immorality or evil, but in reality, an act of sin is anything that is done independently from God. For example, eating fruit is not something we would normally consider evil or sinful; it was the selfish motive of Adam in opposition to God's will that made it so. Independence is a problem because it is the opposite of trusting and obeying God and depending upon Him.

The seeming desirability of independence is one aspect of the deceitfulness of sin; another deception is denying that any action can be of an unrighteous quality. An unrighteous act cannot necessarily be recognized by observation. Many doers of good deeds will stand at the white throne judgment and learn that their "goodness" was produced by the flesh and was not of an acceptable quality to God (Rev 20:11-15). Other doers of good works will be saved, but at the Bema judgment, their deeds will be burned (1 Cor 3:15; Heb 6:8). In both cases, the "good deeds" were done while operating in the flesh; their works might have looked good on the outside, but they were tainted by unrighteous motives, such as the hope of gain or for the sake of a godly appearance. Only by learning to determine one's spiritual condition and to operate as a spiritual man—by grace through faith in the promises of God to the Church—can a Christian produce works which are of an acceptable quality. Only God can produce good works because only God is good.

Chapter Two

The Swamp of the Flesh

KEY CONCEPTS:

- **Carnality, also known as fleshliness, is one of two spiritual conditions possible for a Christian.**
- **The enemy known as the flesh affects the mind with temptation and unrighteousness in thought or motive.**
- **When fleshliness leads to a sinful act, this is known as a "work of the flesh."**
- **Christians who recognize the tendencies of their own flesh can put away fleshly thinking before a work of the flesh manifests.**

"The flesh" is a term coined by Paul to refer to the human body under the influence of sin. The most easily understood aspect of this enemy is the *works* of the flesh. Works of the flesh are the obviously ungodly actions which outwardly portray the inward condition of carnality; they are *acts* of sin.

Because sin dwells in the body, one might associate carnality (aka fleshliness) only with the desires of the body. But sin influences the mind as well (Ro 8:5; Eph 2:3; Col 2:18). The Bible describes several aspects of fleshliness including unrighteousness, a fleshly mind, and erring in the heart, meaning a poor decision. These terms refer to the fact that not only our actions, but our ideas and decisions can also be of an ungodly quality, even if they do not lead to an act of sin. The flesh influences the creation of many products, such as unrighteous motives, impure thoughts, or toying with the idea of following through with a temptation.

In order to live in spiritual freedom from the power of sin, a saint must be familiar with the various facets of his own sinful nature. This awareness enables him to quickly recognize a fleshly craving, whether mental or physical, and mortify it, meaning to count himself dead to the temptation to sin before it leads to an act of sin (Ro 6:11, 8:13; Col 3:5; 1 Pet 2:24). In doing so, he might say to himself, "I know that Christ has made me free. Because God's word says so, I believe it, and I do not have to follow through with this. I know that God's will for me is better than what I am tempted by."

Every moment in the life of a Christian contains a choice to live in the freedom that he has in Christ or in bondage under the dominion of the "law of sin," a manner of operation that is energized by one's sinful nature. When a Christian produces a work of the flesh, he is being ruled by the law of sin within him. This means that he is quenching the work of the Holy Spirit and has returned to operating in his own power, just as he did when he was a natural (unsaved) man. This mode of operation will be explained in detail in the following chapters.

Manifestations of the Flesh

Now the works of the flesh are manifest... (Gal 5:19a)

What Paul calls the "works of the flesh" are the visible manifestations of the law of sin. A Christian's spiritual condition is not always evident, but these easily recognizable products of the flesh are conclusive evidence of carnality. For example, nobody can commit murder "as to the Lord." The act of murder leaves no doubt that the perpetrator was motivated by sin.

The law of sin is always at work in the members (parts) of the human body. A Christian must know himself well enough to recognize it when it asserts itself and reckon himself free from it before it becomes a work of the flesh. The Christian who persists in the sin-empowered condition known as carnality will eventually manifest one or more of the works of the flesh.

Paul's letter to the Galatians contains significant information about carnality. In short, the members of the Galatian church knew they had been saved by grace, but allowed someone to convince them to add some "do and don'ts" to their Christian life. In adding law, they had abandoned the grace-through-faith power of the Spirit and had returned to operating by the law of sin in the flesh.

Are ye so foolish? having begun in the Spirit, are ye now made perfect (mature) *by the flesh?* (Gal 3:3, synonym added)

This syncretic philosophy amounted to a denial of the sufficiency of grace, which operates only as *grace alone*. Through faith, grace accesses the power of God which is required to produce and maintain holy living. Because law of any kind has no intrinsic power to prevent sin, the Galatians quickly became carnal. Paul provided them with examples of how the law of sin manifests itself and reminded them that no law can oppose the power of the Spirit: God's system works every time—if we use it (Gal 5:23). The Galatian believers needed to choose which operating system they were going to use: a law system powered by the flesh or the power of God's grace activated by faith.

The Galatians Chapter Five list of fleshly works includes the phrase, "and such like," meaning that the list is representative, not exhaustive. Each Christian must make himself aware of the character of his own flesh so that he might recognize it when a temptation to sin arises.

> *Now the works of the flesh are **manifest**, which are* these; *Adultery, fornication, uncleanness, lasciviousness, Idolatry, witchcraft, hatred, variance, emulations, wrath, strife, seditions, heresies, Envyings, murders, drunkenness, revellings, **and such like**: of the which I tell you before, as I have also told* you *in time past, that they which do such things shall not inherit the kingdom of God.* (Gal 5:19-21)

Following is a brief description of the items in the list, excluding the easily understood murder, marital adultery, and drunkenness.

Fornication: any sexual behavior outside of marriage.

Uncleanness: impurity, whether physically, morally, or mentally—as in a dirty mind or impure motives; the poor condition of living which results from immorality; defilement. This could include the impure misuse of marital relations (Heb 13:4).

Lasciviousness: shamelessness; a wide variety of behaviors resulting from a shameless attitude, such as making a spectacle of oneself in front of others.

Idolatry: any desire for things which are above one's desire for God and His word. (Col 3:5)

Witchcraft: this is the word for "pharmacy," and refers to "religious awe." It originated in the use of drugs to create a religious experience, hence showing both to be fleshly—the desire for an altered state, as well as the self-centered desire to gain an experience or feeling from one's religious practice. It can be non-drug related religious activity for self-gratification, rather than for the purpose of reinforcing biblical wisdom and knowledge (Col 3:16) or for acknowledging to God the perfection of His character and works.

Hatred: hostility, opposition, lack of sacrificial love, the opposite of being a friend.

Variance: debate and contentiousness rather than teachability; strife rather than peace; wrangling with others—as in making relationships difficult; quarrelsome; "gotcha." (Note: fleshliness can arise in a particular situation and may not necessarily characterize a person's demeanor in general.)

Emulations: this is the Greek word for "zeal," and refers to a jealous rivalry, a competitiveness to beat or best someone else. It is also translated as indignation or envy with the different shades of meaning implied by those words. Sometimes the word refers to godly zeal, an enthusiasm for doing godly works (Titus 2:14). Even this can be twisted by the law of sin to be fleshly when there is an enthusiasm to do a "good" thing "for God," but in ignorance (Ro 10:2). The vast majority of "good works" done by churches today appear to be of this type as they do not conform to the clear instructions given to the Church. The difference between godly zeal and fleshly zeal is the source—either the Holy Spirit or the law of sin.

Wrath: a hot anger, rage, boiling over.

Strife: not a good translation; this word means self-promotion, putting yourself first, trying to get your way, self-will. In secular usage it is political partisanship, electioneering, and party-making, as in getting followers for yourself or your ideas.

Seditions: to stand apart, cause division or dissension.

Heresies: from the idea of choosing, as in choosing to believe something other than what the scripture teaches.

Envyings: this is the word that we would normally think of as envy, to want something for oneself that someone else has; jealousy. (In the KJV, the word "zeal" is sometimes translated envy, but in those cases, it is not just a desire to have, but means the desire to deprive someone else of what they have, according to *Vine's Complete Expository Dictionary*.)

Revellings: carousing, partying, rioting, "cutting loose;" revelry often includes drunkenness.

The Shades of Fleshliness

There are many more works of the flesh described in the scriptures. Galatians Chapter Five is simply a good place to begin its study. This list might seem irrelevant; perhaps you cannot even imagine a situation in which you would murder someone. But you may have felt anger that is of the same *quality* as a murderous rage, even if you never said a word. Maybe it wasn't that intense, but it certainly wasn't the spiritual condition of love, joy, and peace. Perhaps you would never get drunk, but you look forward to that one drink quite often; your relief after a hard day is not in the pure gold of God's word, but in a glass, bottle, or can. Maybe you are convinced that you cannot be friendly or kind in the morning until you have had your preferred morning beverage; it is the object of your faith to produce a good attitude. The works of the flesh are not defined by their intensity, but by their motive, quality, and source.

There are no laws for Christians against food or beverages; that is not the issue here. The issue is that to live in spiritual freedom, a Christian must be able to recognize the operation of the flesh and the assumptions he makes about what constitutes carnality. In most American Christians, the works of the flesh are not going to manifest as total degradation or wickedness. The flesh, however mildly it is displayed, is free to reign within us when we go through the motions of life without discerning our attitudes, words, and actions. Things such as our choices of drink, for example, prove our *true conviction* regarding the soothing of the soul and the refreshing of the spirit. Every Christian, whether he is the esteemed leader of a church or the most down-and-out saint you know, moment by moment, is either trusting in the sufficient power of God's word or in a flesh-inspired fix.

> *All things are lawful unto me, but all things are not expedient: all things are lawful for me, but I will not be brought under the power of any.* (1 Cor 6:12; see also 1 Cor 10:23)

And Now We Have This Issue...

A few decades ago, America climbed onto the slippery slope in regard to human sexuality. As American culture has become dissolute—even in regard to the most perverse permutations of immorality—some elements within the Church seem to wink at the more mundane manifestations of sexual sin. As the greater culture has become more wicked, other sins might seem to pale in comparison. For example, while some forms of fornication are still known to be evil, others seem to be considered mere "slip-ups;" a cohabiting Christian doesn't seem so bad when compared to allowing male predators in the girl's bathroom. God's attitude toward any kind of sin, however, has not changed. We must believe the promises of God to keep us free from both sin and fleshly thinking, and not be drawn into compromise. Compromise is all around us now, but spirituality has no middle ground; every Christian in every moment is either spiritual or carnal and there is no third option.

> *Having therefore these promises, dearly beloved, let us cleanse ourselves from all filthiness of the flesh and spirit, perfecting holiness in the fear of God.* (2 Cor 7:1; see also 2 Pet 2:18-19)

Do All Things as to The Lord

The same is true for the ordinary struggles of life—we are either operating by the power of God or by the law of sin. For example, we can't scream at our kids "as to the Lord," but neither can we quietly mutter complaints under our breath as a spiritual man. We can't honor God with an impatient, sarcastic response to our spouse, nor screaming alone in the car at the driver ahead of us, but all things are to be done as if we are doing them for the Lord, Himself (Eph 6:7; Col 3:23). Our spiritual condition matters to God, no matter what we are doing, or whether anyone else knows.

One's spiritual condition results in behavior, but it begins with motive and attitude. When tempted to think, "But that's not me," here is God's response:

> *If we say that we have no sin* (referring to the law of sin),
> *we deceive ourselves, and the truth is not* (operating) *in us.*
> (1 Jhn 1:8, clarification added)

Therefore thou art inexcusable, O man, whosoever thou art that judgest: for wherein thou judgest another, thou condemnest thyself; for thou that judgest doest the same things. (Ro 2:1)

If we downplay our unrighteous character traits, we will not be open to correction or be able to use the saving power of grace which is available for daily living. If our thoughts and beliefs progressively come into alignment with the trajectory of this evil age (Gal 1:4), it becomes increasingly difficult to correct ourselves. More doubts will enter, more attacks will come, and more compromises will be made. Each Christian must take time to review the quality of his internal condition, and not excuse himself on the "mild" sins or even the thoughts, feelings, and motives that lead to them. If he does not do so, more carnality will manifest, as proven publicly by the many fallen ministers who harbored unrighteous thoughts, eventually worked them out, and then were found out. Most Christians will probably not ever get that far into the works of the flesh, but God is just as dishonored with an unrighteous thought as He is with a sinful act. It was the *intention* of Adam to disobey that broke spiritual fellowship with God. He committed an offense before he disobeyed. A careful reading of Romans Chapter Five reveals that he was condemned *before* he became a sinner by his action; spiritual victory begins in the mind.

*Therefore as by the **offence** of one judgment came *upon all men to **condemnation***; even so by the righteousness of one the free gift came *upon all men unto justification of life. For as by one man's **disobedience** many were made **sinners**, so by the obedience of one shall many be made righteous.* (Ro 5:18-19)

It is not Hopeless

Every Christian is carnal at times. Some of us might recognize that in "just being ourselves" we are probably carnal more often than not. This does not mean we are evil, wicked, or perverse. It simply means that we are not checking in with God frequently regarding our inward condition, and are, therefore, operating by the power of our flesh—and it feels natural to do so. I might think, "I'm just doing my job!" So I am, but am I partnering with God in doing so? Is He near to my thoughts so as to ward off a sudden attack of the flesh when something goes wrong? Is the quality of my mind unruffled, knowing that God provides all I need? I must ask myself such things so as to allow the Holy Spirit to bring to remembrance the truths which enable me to walk as a spiritual man (Jhn 14:26).

A foundational part of maturing in Christ is to recognize an attack of the flesh so that a work of the flesh is not manifested. This is something that we all are equipped to do, and God is always available to help us with it. His word emanates His beautiful character, and as we feed upon it as the vital food our spirit craves, our reactions and responses will become more Christlike. Our minds will be unruffled, filled with gratitude, love, and confident expectation. Instead of being stuck in the swamp of the flesh, we will rejoice in the unsearchable riches of God's grace and that great hope—the return of our Savior. We will mature.

O the depth of the riches both of the wisdom and knowledge of God! (Ro 11:33a)

In whom we have redemption through his blood, the forgiveness of sins, according to the riches of his grace; (Eph 1:7)

The eyes of your understanding being enlightened; that ye may know what is the hope of his calling, and what the riches of the glory of his inheritance in the saints… (Eph 1:18)

That in the ages to come he might shew the exceeding riches of his grace in his *kindness toward us through Christ Jesus.* (Eph 2:7)

Unto me, who am less than the least of all saints, is this grace given, that I should preach among the Gentiles the unsearchable riches of Christ; (Eph 3:8)

But my God shall supply all your need according to his riches in glory by Christ Jesus. (Phil 4:19)

To whom God would make known what is *the riches of the glory of this mystery among the Gentiles; which is Christ in you, the hope of glory:* (Col 1:27)

That their hearts might be comforted, being knit together in love, and unto all riches of the full assurance of understanding, to the acknowledgement of the mystery of God, and of the Father, and of Christ; (Col 2:2)

Looking for that blessed hope, and the glorious appearing of the great God and our Saviour Jesus Christ; (Titus 2:13)

Finally, brethren, whatsoever things are true, whatsoever things are *honest, whatsoever things* are *just, whatsoever things* are *pure, whatsoever things* are *lovely, whatsoever things* are *of good report; if* there be *any virtue, and if* there be *any praise, think on these things.* (Phil 4:8)

Romans 8:1-13

1 There is therefore now no condemnation to them which are in Christ Jesus, who walk not after the flesh, but after the Spirit. 2 For the law of the Spirit of life in Christ Jesus hath made me free from the law of sin and death. 3 For what the law could not do, in that it was weak through the flesh, God sending his own Son in the likeness of sinful flesh, and for sin, condemned sin in the flesh: 4 That the righteousness of the law might be fulfilled in us, who walk not after the flesh, but after the Spirit. 5 For they that are after the flesh do mind the things of the flesh; but they that are after the Spirit the things of the Spirit. 6 For to be carnally minded is death; but to be spiritually minded is life and peace. 7 Because the carnal mind is enmity against God: for it is not subject to the law of God, neither indeed can be. 8 So then they that are in the flesh cannot please God. 9 But ye are not in the flesh, but in the Spirit, if so be that the Spirit of God dwell in you. Now if any man have not the Spirit of Christ, he is none of his. 10 And if Christ be in you, the body is dead because of sin; but the Spirit is life because of righteousness. 11 But if the Spirit of him that raised up Jesus from the dead dwell in you, he that raised up Christ from the dead shall also quicken your mortal bodies by his Spirit that dwelleth in you. 12 Therefore, brethren, we are debtors, not to the flesh, to live after the flesh. 13 For if ye live after the flesh, ye shall die: but if ye through the Spirit do mortify the deeds of the body, ye shall live.

Chapter Three

The Law of Sin in the Flesh

KEY CONCEPTS:

- The law of sin is the motivating force within every person which moves them to oppose God.
- One must be born again and filled with the Spirit (spiritual) in order to do anything in the way which is pleasing to God.
- To return to spirituality from carnality in Christian living, a Christian must change his mind and return to agreement with God in regard to his sin.
- Spirituality is attained/regained by reckoning true that God has freed us from sin and believing His promises to produce His character in us.

God has promised spiritual freedom to His children. He can do so because Jesus paid for all the sins of the world. Those who believe the Gospel, 1 Corinthians 15:1-4, have been made free from both the penalty of sin and the power of sin. But every Christian has sin dwelling within him and can succumb at any time. To live in spiritual freedom, a Christian must have some understanding of his own sinful nature which naturally opposes and operates independently from God. The saint who recognizes it when it asserts itself can use the power of God's grace to reject the temptation to sin. To succumb to temptation, even in seemingly small things such as sharp remarks, overeating, or breaking a traffic law, is to operate by the power of the law (principle) of sin and dishonor God. Such a statement is not legalism; this issue is a matter of whether one is operating by grace through faith, or its only alternative—sin (Ro 14:23).

Terminology

Paul refers to sin as a law because he is describing the way in which something works, similarly to when someone uses the phrase "the law of gravity," or "the law of supply and demand." The law of sin can also be called the principle of sin, or sin principle, terms which help to differentiate it from "the Law," meaning the Law of Moses. To operate by the law of sin is the natural condition of fallen mankind. When Paul is referring to the source of sin, he calls it the "flesh," coining a particular usage of that word.

Every mention of "flesh" in the epistles is not according to Paul's unique use of the term; the word might simply be referring to some aspect of physical life, such as the physical body (2 Cor 12:7) or a family relationship (Ro 9:3), for example. The meaning of "flesh" must be determined by context. Familiarity with the various terms relating to the law of sin are helpful when studying it.

Law of sin: An operating principle and a motivating power for the natural man and the carnal man. Using it is to operate contrary to God's will. It is also referred to (less precisely) as the sin nature. Human nature is sinful, but there is not a "thing" in us called the "sin nature." This distinction is important for the sake of learning that there are two "operating systems" or "power sources" available for Christians to use. Using the law of sin is a way of living, and unlike the natural man, Christians have a choice to use it or to be spiritual.

Flesh: The source and dwelling place of the law of sin; the body under the dominion of the law of sin, a spiritual enemy.

Carnal: One's spiritual condition when using the law of sin; the lack of the Spirit-filled condition. It is a reference to the realm of the physical. This condition is also described as "soulish," a word that is translated "natural" or "sensual" in the King James Version of the Bible. Soulish refers to the fact that the second part of the mind and the seat of volition—the human soul—is being influenced by the flesh rather than by God. (1 Pet 2:11)

Law of God after the inward man: This is the grace-through-faith operating principle of the spiritual man. It is exactly the opposite of the law of sin: It originates in the human spirit, not the body, and it operates in dependence upon God, not in independence from God. The inward (or inner) man refers to the non-physical part of man, the mind. For that reason, Paul also refers to this law as the "law of the mind." When using this principle, the regenerated human spirit is directing the soul (volition). In the carnal man, the flesh is directing the soul. (See Chapter One diagrams.)

Members: Human body parts. The law of sin is said to operate "in the members" (Ro 7:5, 23).

Carnality originates in the human body, which is thoroughly and permanently infested by the law of sin. The members of the body will never be clean from sin as long as we live on this earth; we must have a new body that is free from sin in order to enter into God's presence.

> *For I know that in me (that is, in my flesh,) dwelleth no good thing…* (Ro 7:18a)

> *Who shall change our vile body, that it may be fashioned like unto his glorious body…* (Phil 3:21a)

Nothing Apart from God is Good

Although it is often called the "sin nature," the Bible calls sin a law; it is a way of operating. The law or principle of sin is the singular energizing force within the natural (unsaved) man; he can operate in no other way. The law of sin dwells in the members of every human body, moving both sinners and unsuspecting saints to fulfill their desires.

> *For when ye were the servants of sin, ye were free from righteousness.* (Ro 6:20)

> *Among whom also we all had our conversation in times past in the lusts of our flesh, fulfilling the desires of the flesh and of the mind; and were by nature the children of wrath, even as others.* (Eph 2:3)

The sinfulness of every human being can be observed even in very young children: they must be taught to obey their parents, to share, to listen, to sit still, and many other things. They will lie, disobey, and act selfishly without ever being taught to do so or even observing such things. Although a person can choose to act rightly according to societal standards or other authorities, his operating system continues to be the law of sin until he is saved from sin by faith in the Gospel of Christ.

*For when we were in the flesh, the motions of sins, which were by the law, did work in our members to bring forth fruit unto death. **But now** we are delivered from the law, that being dead wherein we were held; that we should serve in newness of spirit, and not in the oldness of the letter.* (Ro 7:5-6)

Because sins are actions, and every act of man is done in his body, all the actions of a natural man are fouled by the law of sin; therefore, nothing he does pleases God. In God's estimation, everything done by the natural man falls short of His perfect and holy standard. Even when the natural man intends to do rightly and his works appear to be good and even selfless in the estimation of others, his motives remain selfish: he might be proud, pleased with himself, and eager to reap the rewards of his good works. He might think himself humble, but he counts his humility to be good. He is self-righteous in even presuming to be good or to have done something good apart from God. Therefore, from the viewpoint of God's perfect Law, there is "none that doeth good, no not one" (Ro 3:12; Ps 14:1-3, 53:1-3). Every man in his natural state remains spiritually separated from God, regardless of his good intentions or religious works. His human spirit must be washed clean by regeneration (Titus 3:5) so that God can indwell him and commune with him there. God's presence gives spiritual life.

And if Christ be in you, the body is dead because of sin; but the Spirit is life because of righteousness. But if the Spirit of him that raised up Jesus from the dead dwell in you, he that raised up Christ from the dead shall also quicken your mortal bodies by his Spirit that dwelleth in you. (Ro 8:10-11)

Because the human bodies of the saints remain tainted by sin, they are called "dead" in verse 10, meaning separated from God.

The spiritual life imparted to those who believe the Gospel is the reason for calling salvation a new birth. Salvation is a spiritual birth that ends the separation between God and man, and provides access to the power that raised Jesus from the dead! After death, the saints' new bodies will be forever free of sin and fit for life in God's presence.

> *But there shall by no means enter it anything that defiles, or causes an abomination or a lie, but only those who are written in the Lamb's Book of Life.* (Rev 21:27 NKJV)

Salvation Provides a Choice

Every human being operates only according to the law of sin until he is delivered from its power through faith in the Gospel of Christ, 1 Corinthians 15:1-4. There is no other operating principle available for the natural (unsaved) man; he is not indwelt by God and can only operate "in the flesh," a reference to his physical body indwelt and controlled by the law of sin.

> *For when we were in the flesh, the motions of sins, which were by the law, did work in our members to bring forth fruit unto death.* (Ro 7:5)

One's initial faith in the death, burial, and resurrection of Jesus Christ for sins provides not only deliverance from damnation, but also the energizing power of God's grace to live differently: the spiritual life of the new birth enables obedience to God through daily faith in the promises of God. God does not tell us to do things that we cannot; He equips us to deal with life as spiritual men. To obey the instructions in the letters to the Church is to live out the present salvation from daily sin, a benefit which belongs to each believer.

Wherefore, my beloved, as ye have always obeyed, not as in
my presence only, but now much more in my absence, work
out your own salvation with fear and trembling. (Phil 2:12)

Christians are to learn the promises of God to the church and believe them. To do so is to operate by faith, which is to be the normal operating principle of Christian living. The only other operating principle that exists is the law of sin.

*But **without faith** it is **impossible to please** him: for he*
that cometh to God must believe that he is, and that *he is a*
rewarder of them that diligently seek him. (Heb 11:6)

And he that doubteth is damned if he eat, because he eateth
*not of faith: for **whatsoever** is **not of faith is sin**.* (Ro 14:23)

5 *For they that are after the flesh do mind the things of the*
flesh; but they that are after the Spirit the things of the Spirit.
For to be carnally minded is *death; but to be spiritually*
minded is *life and peace. Because the carnal mind* is *enmity*
against God: for it is not subject to the law of God, neither
*indeed can be. So **then they that are in the flesh cannot***
please God. (Ro 8:5-8)

As ye have therefore received Christ Jesus the Lord (by faith)*,*
so walk ye in him (by faith)*:* (Col 2:6, clarification added)

The sin principle operates within the physical body of every living person, even after one is saved. Just as God does not force people to accept the Gospel, neither does He force Christians to cooperate with Him; therefore, any Christian is capable of carnality, operating as if he is still a natural (unsaved) man. The carnal Christian has chosen to cooperate with his sinful nature, even though he has the option of being spiritual. The spiritual man does not obey the law of sin in the members of his body, but sets his mind upon the truths that make him free.

> *And ye shall know the truth, and the truth shall make you free.* (Jhn 8:32)

> *For though we walk in the flesh, we do not war after the flesh: (For the weapons of our warfare* are *not carnal* (physical), *but mighty through God to the pulling down of strong holds;) Casting down imaginations* (reasoning contrary to a good conscience), *and every high thing that exalteth itself against the knowledge of God, and bringing into captivity **every thought** to the obedience of Christ;* (2 Cor 10:3-5, clarification added)

A Christian who wishes to obey God might say to himself, "I feel like I cannot do this, but God's word calls me to do it. That means God will enable me, and I believe it." Each saint who learns to recognize his present spiritual condition and intentionally operate by faith can live in accordance with God's will. The more time he spends rehearsing the doctrines of grace, the less likely it is that his soul will be swayed by temptation.

> *But each one is tempted when he is drawn away by his own desires and enticed. … Therefore lay aside all filthiness and overflow of wickedness, and receive with meekness the implanted word, which is able to save your souls* (from temptation). (Ja 1:14, 21 NKJV, clarification added)

Recovering from Carnality

Every Christian is carnal at times because every Christian sins. When a Christian sins, he is operating by the law of sin in his flesh rather than by reckoning himself free from sin. The conditions of spirituality and carnality originate in different places within us. Spirituality originates in the human spirit, the place where God dwells. The spirit has been made a clean place for fellowship (aka communion) with God. The spiritual man is sometimes referred to as being "in fellowship."

When a saint is operating "in the flesh," he is also "out of fellowship" with God. He has not lost his eternal salvation, but he is not using it; he is quenching the operation of the Holy Spirit within him. Rather than using the power of God's grace to display the virtues of Christ, he is "being himself," doing what comes naturally, and using his own power—the energizing power of the law of sin. What he says or does in this condition may or may not seem wicked from the perspective of human judgment, but it is not of an acceptable quality to God. Therefore, *functionally*, the relationship with God is broken until the saint repents—meaning he changes his mind about his condition and returns to faith in the promises of God to produce Christlikeness within him. Christian repentance is a specific change of mind: it is "confession," a word which means to say the same thing. In other words, the saint is now willing to say the same thing about his condition as God says about it. He has abandoned his false view regarding sin ("It's not that bad." "That's just how I am." "I needed to." "I had to say something.") and has returned to agreement with God. Nothing else is required to return to fellowship; it is a purely spiritual, internal transaction between the believer and the Lord.

"That's Just Me."

Sometimes fleshly operation is accompanied with a deception such as, "This is just the way I am. I cannot do otherwise." Or "I didn't mean to; it's just a habit." Human wisdom often reinforces such beliefs with claims such as someone being "born that way," "raised that way," or having a "disease" which is actually a behavior or a false belief. Such an "explanation" is simply another form of rebellion against the truth of God's word. Yes, there are many reasons for sin, but there are no excuses. Behavior is a choice. Ignorance is also a choice. Non-Christians must be born again. Christians have been made free from the power of sin and must study, learn, and use the doctrines of grace in order to live accordingly.

> *Examine yourselves, whether ye be* (operating*) in the faith; prove your own selves. Know ye not your own selves, how that Jesus Christ is* (operating) *in you, except ye be reprobates?* (2 Cor 13:5, clarification added)

> *What? know ye not that your body is the temple of the Holy Ghost which is in you, which ye have of God, and ye are not your own?* (1 Cor 6:19)

Nothing is too Big for God

God's written word is living and active, providing spiritual power to deliver the saints from both the penalty and the power of sin (Ro 1:16). God's power raised Jesus from the dead; this source of strength is proclaimed throughout the epistles and is able to conquer the law of sin, no matter what form it takes. The Christian life is a continual series of choices, beginning with the choice to learn how spiritual life operates. From there, choices are day-by-day and even moment-by-moment. When facing temptation, the Christian can reckon himself dead to it rather than succumb. Practices such as taking a moment before answering others, renewing the mind with truth, and evaluating one's motives can proactively protect us, keeping us from even getting to the point of being tempted to sin. Through self-examination and time in God's word, each Christian can learn to utilize God's provisions. As we come to know God better, our faith in His promises will grow; we will enjoy more consistent victory over the swamp of the flesh, thereby glorifying God and honoring Christ's sacrifice which freed us from bondage to sin.

> *...I...Cease not to give thanks for you, making mention of you in my prayers; That the God of our Lord Jesus Christ, the Father of glory, may give unto you the spirit of wisdom and revelation in the knowledge of him: The eyes of your understanding being enlightened; that ye may know what is the hope of his calling, and what the riches of the glory of his inheritance in the saints, And what* is *the exceeding greatness of his power to us-ward who believe, according to the working of his **mighty power, Which he wrought in Christ, when he raised him from the dead,** and set* him *at his own right hand in the heavenly* places... (Eph 1:16-20)

> *Strengthened with all **might**, according to his **glorious power**, unto all patience and longsuffering with joyfulness*; (Col 1:11)

> *Wherefore also we pray always for you, that our God would count* you *worthy of this calling, and fulfil all the good pleasure of* his *goodness, and **the work of faith with power***: (2 Thes 1:11)

> *According as his **divine power** hath given unto us **all things** that* pertain *unto life and godliness, through the **knowledge** of him that hath called us to glory and virtue*: (2 Pet 1:3)

Romans 7:1-11

1 Know ye not, brethren, (for I speak to them that know the law,) how that the law hath dominion over a man as long as he liveth? 2 For the woman which hath an husband is bound by the law to her husband so long as he liveth; but if the husband be dead, she is loosed from the law of her husband. 3 So then if, while her husband liveth, she be married to another man, she shall be called an adulteress: but if her husband be dead, she is free from that law; so that she is no adulteress, though she be married to another man. 4 Wherefore, my brethren, ye also are become dead to the law by the body of Christ; that ye should be married to another, even to him who is raised from the dead, that we should bring forth fruit unto God. 5 For when we were in the flesh, the motions of sins, which were by the law, did work in our members to bring forth fruit unto death. 6 But now we are delivered from the law, that being dead wherein we were held; that we should serve in newness of spirit, and not in the oldness of the letter. 7 What shall we say then? Is the law sin? God forbid. Nay, I had not known sin, but by the law: for I had not known lust, except the law had said, Thou shalt not covet. 8 But sin, taking occasion by the commandment, wrought in me all manner of concupiscence. For without the law sin was dead. 9 For I was alive without the law once: but when the commandment came, sin revived, and I died. 10 And the commandment, which was ordained to life, I found to be unto death. 11 For sin, taking occasion by the commandment, deceived me, and by it slew me.

Chapter Four

Understanding the Nature of Law: Romans 7:1-11

KEY CONCEPTS

- **Christians are free from the Law of Moses and free from the law of sin.**
- **Law is a trigger for sin.**
- **Israel's failure to keep the Law showed mankind its need for a savior from sin.**
- **Grace does not make us free to sin; it makes us free *not* to sin.**

Romans Chapter Seven is the equivalent of a technical manual on the operation of the law (principle) of sin, including Paul's personal testimony of how he was deceived by it. Its base of operation, how it defeats the well-intentioned but ignorant Christian, and its alternative—the law of God after the inward man—are all described in Romans Chapter Seven. From his own experience, Paul details his failure when trying to live the Christian life in conjunction with law. His attempt to incorporate the Law of Moses as an enhancement to spirituality immediately resulted in carnality. Paul's good intention to improve his Christian life actually destroyed it, because adding law-keeping required a shift from unquestioning faith in the sufficiency of God's grace to Paul's own personal resolve to obey a rule.

Marriage as an Example of Law: Romans 7:1-4

Know ye not, brethren, (for I speak to them that know the law,) how that the law hath dominion over a man as long as he liveth? For the woman which hath an husband is bound by the law to her husband so long as he liveth; but if the husband be dead, she is loosed from the law of her husband. So then if, while her husband liveth, she be married to another man, she shall be called an adulteress: but if her husband be dead, she is free from that law; so that she is no adulteress, though she be married to another man. (Ro 7:1-3; see also 1 Cor 7:39)

Laws of all sorts govern the lives of men. Paul introduces the internal battle with the sin principle by using marriage and widowhood as examples of living according to law. Marital laws are intended to bind together husband and wife as long as both parties live. Naturally, when one party dies, the other is no longer bound by the laws of marriage. Through death, widows and widowers have been removed from their position as a husband or wife. Similarly, through his spiritual baptism into Christ described in Romans Chapter Six, a believer is removed from his position "in Adam" and placed into a new position in the spiritual entity known as the body of Christ. The believer is then to learn how to live in accordance with this new reality.

In Romans 7:4, Paul transitions to the new "marriage" into which the believer has entered. The product of this marriage is spiritual fruit.

> *Wherefore, my brethren, ye also are become dead to the law by the body of Christ; that ye should be married to another, even to him who is raised from the dead, that we should bring forth fruit unto God.* (Ro 7:4)

Upon faith in the Gospel of Christ, 1 Corinthians 15:1-4, a Christian is made free. He is counted by God to be both dead to sin and dead to the law; he is no longer under the dominion of either and is no longer bound to sin. The law of sin within him is not dead: the Christian is to live dead *to it.* This means that in regard to any temptation to sin, the Christian is to respond to it as if he himself is dead. A dead man is not tempted to sin; he is free from temptation. Likewise, when one's spouse dies, the one who lives is dead in regard to the laws of marriage; he or she is free from it.

> *For the law of the Spirit of life in Christ Jesus hath made me free from the law of sin and death.* (Ro 8:2)

> *Who his own self bare our sins in his own body on the tree, that we, **being dead to sins**, should live unto righteousness: by whose stripes ye were healed* (from those sins). (1 Pet 2:24, clarification added)

Being dead to the law of the previous marriage is necessary for the new marriage. Using this analogy, Paul shows that the Christian must count himself dead to sin and dead to the law in order to bear the fruit of spirituality, something which God intends for every believer.

The Motivation to Sin: Romans 7:5-6

For when we were (operating) *in the flesh* (unsaved), *the motions of sins,* **which were by the law,** *did work in our members to bring forth fruit unto death* (separation from God). *But now we are delivered from the law, that being dead wherein we were held; that we should serve in newness of spirit, and not* in *the oldness of the letter.* (Ro 7:5-6, clarification added.)

In the mind of God, Christians are identified with Christ's death and burial; therefore, we are dead to our former position as captives to sin and death. Even so, serving in the "oldness of the letter" (the letter of the written Law), remains a possibility for the Christian; that is the reason for Paul's warning not to do so but to instead serve in "newness of spirit." Paul had to remind himself that he had been delivered from the Law, under which he was separated from God until all sins were paid by Christ on the cross. After the resurrection, a new way of life was revealed—a new birth which enabled spiritual power for holy living and service to God.

A Christian who is operating by using rules or law of any kind is not functioning as a spiritual believer, because he is being motivated from the wrong source. For example, imagine a person responding to a traffic signal, a no trespassing sign, or his teacher's rule of no chewing gum in class. These external commands have no empowerment mechanism to enable compliance. A person might decide to obey to avoid negative consequences, because he appreciates orderly society, out of respect for the rule-maker, or because he is treated better when he acts rightly. Whatever the reason for obedience to rules and laws, the vital point is this: law is an external limit used to coax the flesh into obedience.

It was instituted by God to reveal the impossibility of human righteousness. It is now used by the world to control human sin. Law cannot produce righteousness; a Christian who uses law is shifting from the power of grace to a system utilized by the flesh.

Knowing this, that the law is not made for a righteous man…
(1 Tim 1:9a)

Paul did not write the previous verse to Timothy to say that believers are not subject to law, do not benefit from law, or do not commit unlawful acts. (Consider the church at Corinth.) To the contrary, we are to obey laws and should be grateful to God that they provide order and protection in this fallen world. They are not, however, the proper source of motivation for a Christian. As opposed to an external system that imposes punishment, grace-through-faith is a spiritual system motivated by love. A Christian cannot use both. If he is not using the power of God, he is operating in the flesh as if he is a natural man. He is carnal.

The exclusion of law for Christian living should not be misunderstood as if it means that a Christian is free to sin. The opposite is true: only a spiritual Christian is free *not* to sin! We are not, however, free from temptation. We know from the Romans Chapter Seven context that Paul was coveting something; it seems that he said or did something sinful to gain what he wanted. In Romans 7:5-6, the phrase, "motions of sins," refers to the motivation to disobey God or to act independently from Him. The phrase includes the idea of an external influence, and in Paul's example of covetousness, that influence came "by the law." It was the law that facilitated Paul's carnality! But the Bible states that the law is good (Ro 7:12, 16; 1 Tim 1:8). It displayed God's holiness and made Israel distinctive among the nations. So how can something good also be a motivation to sin, which is evil? The answer lies in another purpose of the law: the knowledge of sin.

> *Therefore by the deeds of the law there shall no flesh be justified in his sight: for by the law is the knowledge of sin.* (Ro 3:20)

Leveraging the Law: Romans 7:7-11

> *What shall we say then? Is the law sin? God forbid. Nay, I had not known sin, but by the law: for I had not known lust, except the law had said, Thou shalt not covet. But sin, taking occasion by the commandment, wrought in me all manner of concupiscence* (strong desire). *For without the law sin was dead. For I was alive without the law once: but when the commandment came, sin revived, and I died. And the commandment, which was ordained to life, I found to be unto death. For sin,* **taking occasion** *by the commandment, deceived me, and by it slew me.* (Ro 7:7-11, definition added)

Is one to conclude from the previous verses that law is "bad?" No, not at all. The Law of Moses is spiritual, meaning it displays the character of God (Ro 7:14a). Like parents raising their children with rules to teach them right from wrong, the administration of the Mosaic Law enabled the Jewish people to recognize their sinfulness and to know things about God, especially His holiness. It served its purpose: to show mankind its lack of holiness and its need for a savior from sin.

Notice in the previous passage that the sin principle is "taking occasion" by the law. It is using something good to accomplish something that is not good. This is one of the reasons why law is so deceptive. Unlike the system of grace through faith, rules and laws invite acts of sin by tempting people to break them. For example, imagine a friend saying, "Don't look." It immediately tempts one to look! The problem described in this passage was not due to the Law itself but was due to the man. The sinful nature of man is tempted by rules; when restricted, he feels the desire to break them. Because of man's tendency to act independently from God, something good—the Law—also revealed something evil: the heart of man.

> *The heart* is *deceitful above all* things*, and desperately wicked: who can know it?* (Jer 17:9)

Paul had been walking by faith; he was spiritually alive and functioning accordingly. How do we know? It is because he said that using the law "slew" him; if he was referring to a time before his regeneration, he would have already been dead in trespasses and sins and could not be "slain." Paul had been walking by faith, but then he added commandments to his Christian life. He apparently thought it would be an improvement, but what he discovered instead was that it caused spiritual "death," meaning a separation from spiritual fellowship with God. Paul was no longer relating to the promises of God and trusting the sufficiency of grace, but was attempting to police himself with "do and don'ts." The power of sin revived in him so that in daily operation he was separated from God. He had not lost his eternal salvation nor his position in Christ, but in regard to Christian living, he had been slain.

Grace Alone

One must understand the nature of law in order to distinguish it from operating as a spiritual man. Law today is for the unrighteous, to curb the lawlessness of man by using external rules and imposing consequences for disobedience. To believe that it can be used with spirituality is a deception; law of any kind destroys the operation of spiritual life because a person cannot function in two opposing systems at the same time. The motivating drive used by law triggers rebellion. As with Paul, using rules to change behavior can seem like a good and legitimate idea. And we know from the scripture that the Law of Moses is good. The issue under grace, however, is to use the operating system that God intends for today. This is the only way to defeat the enemy known as "the flesh." When God illuminates us to spiritual truth, cleanses our mind, motivates our desires, and empowers our actions, everything that we do honors Him, and our Savior receives the glory for it.

Romans 7:12-25

12 Wherefore the law is *holy, and the commandment holy, and just, and good.* 13 *Was then that which is good made death unto me? God forbid. But sin, that it might appear sin, working death in me by that which is good; that sin by the commandment might become exceeding sinful.* 14 *For we know that the law is spiritual: but I am carnal, sold under sin.* 15 *For that which I do I allow not: for what I would, that do I not; but what I hate, that do I.* 16 *If then I do that which I would not, I consent unto the law that* it is *good.* 17 *Now then it is no more I that do it, but sin that dwelleth in me.* 18 *For I know that in me (that is, in my flesh,) dwelleth no good thing: for to will is present with me; but* how *to perform that which is good I find not.* 19 *For the good that I would I do not: but the evil which I would not, that I do.* 20 *Now if I do that I would not, it is no more I that do it, but sin that dwelleth in me.* 21 *I find then a law, that, when I would do good, evil is present with me.* 22 *For I delight in the law of God after the inward man:* 23 *But I see another law in my members, warring against the law of my mind, and bringing me into captivity to the law of sin which is in my members.* 24 *O wretched man that I am! who shall deliver me from the body of this death?* 25 *I thank God through Jesus Christ our Lord. So then with the mind I myself serve the law of God; but with the flesh the law of sin.*

Chapter Five

Understanding the Conflict: Romans 7:12-25

KEY CONCEPTS

- **The Law of Moses reflected the character of God.**
- **Law can never produce righteousness in man.**
- **Spirituality and law-keeping never co-exist.**

C hapter 4 of this book described the operation of the Law and its effect on a believer's life as taught in Romans 7:1-11. Romans 7:12-25 describes in detail the internal battle that occurs within the believer who tries to mix grace with any other method of self-control. The grace of God is the power source for Christian living; it cannot be used in conjunction with any other system. Adding rules or laws of any kind as a means of godliness is to abandon faith in the sufficiency of God and operate instead by the law of sin. A spiritual man has the mind of Christ and *will* do rightly; he does not need law to do so. Furthermore, law has no enabling power to produce righteousness.

It is noteworthy that throughout Romans Chapter Seven, the Greek phrase "the sin" is translated as "sin;" the English translators seemed not to recognize the significance of the definite article.

Sin is an action, while "the sin" refers to the law of sin. The vital importance of knowing whether a verse is teaching about "sin" or "the sin" is that Christians are not free from committing individual acts of sin; because saints are not perfect, all will sin. They have, however, been made free from the dominion of the law of sin: Because of the new birth, Christians are capable of producing something other than sin and no longer *must* sin.

Paul stated in Romans 7:7 that his sin problem was the result of coveting. Perhaps he believed he could not be happy without some change in his situation or some item that he wanted; believing that we cannot be happy without some particular condition in life is a common deception in Christian living. Paul's covetousness led him into carnality, and he had abandoned his freedom. In coveting, his mind was occupied with his own desires, keeping him from the spiritual fruit of contentment (Phil 4:11; 1 Tim 6:6, 8; Heb 13:5). Beginning with Romans 7:12, Paul explains the internal struggle between the law of sin within him and his desire to obey God.

Good Made Bad: Romans 7:12-13a

Romans Chapter Seven explains the operation of the law of sin. In it, Paul continues to expose man's sinfulness using the Law of Moses as the example. He explains that the Law is good, but rather than producing holiness, it leaves man separated from God.

> *Wherefore the law* is *holy, and the commandment holy, and just, and good. Was then that which is good made death* (spiritual separation from fellowship) *unto me? God forbid.* (Ro 7:12-13a, clarification added)

The Law of Moses is good because it reflects the character of God. It is also good in that it reveals right and wrong to man. Man, however, cannot perfectly keep the Law; his flesh is weak. For this reason, operating by using law will never produce righteousness.

For what the law could not do, in that it was weak through the flesh, God sending his own Son in the likeness of sinful flesh, and for sin, condemned sin in the flesh: (Ro 8:3)

To use law of any kind, a Christian must quit the grace-through-faith system of operation and instead use the law of sin. Operating by the law of sin always results in spiritual death (separation from fellowship). This is so, because it is not possible to live in both disobedience and in spiritual fellowship. Christians who try to use law (including personal resolutions, rules, or "do and don'ts") for Christian living separate themselves from fellowship by operating in their own strength. They are using the meager willpower of their sin–tainted flesh rather than yielding to God and operating as spiritual men by faith. On those occasions when their willpower succeeds, it creates pride, not righteousness. Operating in the flesh may not appear overtly evil. But if a Christian is not operating by faith, he cannot please God (Heb 11:6; Ro 8:8, 14:23).

Exceedingly Sinful: Romans 7:13b-15

Paul continues in Romans Chapter Seven with the description of his experience in attempting to live the Christian life by adding law. Although the Law is good, its purpose is to reveal something bad: the sinful nature of man. Therefore, the ultimate result of law-keeping is exceedingly sinful rather than good, because man is not good.

But sin, that it might appear sin, working death in me by that which is good; that sin by the commandment might become exceeding sinful. For we know that the law is spiritual: but I am carnal (fleshly), *sold under sin.* (Ro 7:13b-14, synonym added)

When human nature takes something that is wholly good and produces sin, it is irrefutable proof of the utterly corrupt condition of man and his need for redemption. Our Lord Jesus Christ has redeemed each saint from the slave market of sin. When a Christian operates by way of the Law, he is once again "sold under sin," operating as if he is still in that slave market, and as if he is still "in Adam." Positionally, he is still in Christ, but functionally, he has sold himself back to the dominion of the slave-master of sin rather than operating in the liberty that Christ purchased for him with His own blood. Sometimes it is a completely conscious choice: a person knows that something is sin and yet he does it anyway. In Paul's case, it seems that he had not fully comprehended that the law system can never be mixed with the faith system. He did not want to sin, and in fact hated it, but he had abandoned the resurrection power of grace through faith which enabled him not to sin.

For that which I do I allow not (do not understand): *for what I would, that do I not; but what I hate, that do I.* (Ro 7:15, clarification added)

Not I, But Sin: Romans 7:16-18a

Paul was coveting something that he did not have and perhaps had been telling himself to "Stop it!" by focusing on the commandment that forbids coveting. As he recognized his failure, he realized that he could not blame the Law for his sinful state, but he did not understand why he intended to be good, and yet was not getting the desired result. The Law of Moses was certainly not evil; it reflects the holiness of God.

> *If then I do that which I would not, I consent unto the law that it is good.* (Ro 7:16)

In fact, his failure reminded him that the Law was good, because it highlights sin, and, therefore, the need for deliverance from it. Paul then makes a fascinating distinction between "I" and "sin." He does not equate himself with his sinful human nature:

> *Now then it is no more I* (the person) *that do it, but* (the law of) *sin that dwelleth in me* (my body). *For I know that in me (that is, in my flesh,) dwelleth no good thing…* (Ro 7:17-18a, clarification added)

How can Paul say that it is not he who is sinning? It is because sin is *in* his body, his physical flesh, but Paul's reference to himself—"I"— does not include his thoroughly contaminated body, which will be replaced. According to Paul, the self is comprised of the spirit and soul, those parts of man which live forever. He is a citizen of heaven and his body of sin will not be there (Phil 3:20-21). Sin is a law—it is a way of operating; it is not the equivalent of the person himself.

Paul acknowledges that the principle of sin infests his body; hence, nothing in his body can be counted good. There will be no improvement to his flesh as long as he lives. The law of sin indwells his body, but he himself—the true person consisting of spirit and soul—has been made free from the dominion of sin; his spirit had been washed by regeneration (the new birth) and indwelt by God

(1 Cor 3:16, 6:17, 19). His soul, the seat of volition, can choose to do rightly, in accordance with his salvation (Ja 1:21).

One who has been born again by faith in the Gospel (1 Cor 15:1-4) is counted by God to be righteous (Ro 4:5). He must learn to walk in accordance with God's view of him. Paul's error allowed the sin principle to take advantage of the commandment he tried to follow. This does not absolve him from responsibility for his fall from fellowship. He needed to learn from it, and going forward he would have to remember to intentionally live by faith alone in order to abide in a Spirit-filled condition.

Paul's Dilemma: Romans 7:18b-20

*...for to **will** is present with me; but* how *to perform that which is good I find not. For the good that I would I do not: but the evil which I would not, that I do. Now if I do that I would not, it is no more I that do it, but* (the law of) *sin that dwelleth in me.* (Ro 7:18b-20, clarification added)

In this passage, Paul details the failure of his human will, a function of the soul. James Chapter One describes the soul as divided; it is a sort of "fence-sitter," measuring available choices (Ja 1:6-8). This role of arbiter has been depicted in film, for example, as an angel on one shoulder and a devil on the other. As the seat of volition, the soul either defaults to the law of sin in the flesh, or intentionally aligns with his indwelt human spirit in faith, resulting in spirituality. According to Paul, he wanted to obey God, but could not find the "how" to do it. Having returned to operating by the law of sin, he allowed himself things that he did not want to, and was not able to enjoy spiritual freedom from his desires. The flesh is weak because it cannot use the power of God; it can do no more than use human willpower to tell itself, "No." (Ro 8:3a).

Using means such as rules, laws, commitments, or resolutions is not the answer for behavioral change in a Christian. Think of how famously "New Year's resolutions" fail. Such things both terminate the spiritual operation of a saint and entice him to break the very rule he is using to limit himself. Law does not *in any way* enable Christian living, but instead presents *both the temptation and the method* to operate independently from God. Change comes from faith in God's perfect ability to enable us to be Christlike.

The Source of the Conflict: Romans 7:21-23

Paul's testimony of his bout with carnality in Romans Chapter Seven goes on to describe the two operational systems within himself—one in his body and one in his mind. He is calling Christians to recognize that this is not "just how I am," but it is a *way* of operating that has an alternative. Firstly, he defines the law of sin in the members of his body:

> *I find then a law, that, when I would do good, evil is present with me.* (Ro 7:21)

The law of sin in the flesh is opposed to God. The very thought of doing rightly ignites the oppositional character of the law of sin, according to verse 21. Paul then introduces the second law, calling it "the law of God after the inward man," and "the law of the mind," both of which refer to his non-physical self—his spirit and soul. This second law (principle) is the way in which a believer's mind is to operate, allowing the power of God to change him on the inside.

For I delight in the law of God after the inward man: But I see another law in my members, (the law of sin) *warring against the law of my mind, and bringing me into captivity to the law of sin which is in my members.* (Ro 7:22-23, clarification added)

Paul now recognizes the source of the conflict, and knows that when he aligns his soul (volition) with the godly desires of his regenerated spirit, he experiences delight. His inward man (non-physical self) experiences the freedom of salvation and produces the loving and joyful fruit of spirituality. But the operating principle of his body—the law of sin—is opposed to this. If he does not renew his mind with the applicable truths of Christian living, he will succumb to the law of sin and become a carnal man, captive to sin. He must exercise faith in the grace doctrines of God's word and access its power for living in order to return to spiritual operation.

Paul Figures it Out: Romans 7:24-25

Paul rejoiced in being spiritual and was distressed by his fall into carnality, especially since his intention was to do good by adding a few laws to his Christian life. He longed for deliverance from his sin-infested body which had led to the death of his spiritual life. He answers his own cry for deliverance with the solution that has been provided by his position in Christ. Equating himself again with his mind (his spirit and soul rather than his body), Paul concludes that there are only two possible systems of operation: one that opposes God and one that serves God. He has learned that the law in his mind—the law of God after the inward man—is the sole and sufficient provision by which he can serve God and prevail over the flesh.

O wretched man that I am! who shall deliver me from the
body of this death? I thank God through Jesus Christ our Lord.
So then with the mind I myself serve the law of God (after the
inward man); *but with the flesh the law of sin.* (Ro 7:24-25,
clarification added)

As Paul discovered, sinfulness can co-exist with an intention to
do rightly. This inner contradiction can only be resolved when a
Christian realizes that adding his own efforts to God's ways are
worthless and even detrimental. Paul summarizes what he learned
in Romans 8:1-13, found on page 31 of this book.

Oh, It's Nothing...Or is It?

It is noteworthy that an entire chapter of the Bible was devoted
to something that we might consider mild—wanting something
we don't have. This should emphasize to us the holiness of God,
which counts even that sliver of dissatisfaction as bad as any sin we
might consider heinous. One cannot be dissatisfied and be grateful
to God at the same time, just as one cannot be both spiritual and
carnal. An ungracious tone of voice can cut as deeply as a curse,
and a complaint is an accusation against what God has provided.
To believe that joyfulness, contentment, or freedom from anxiety
is not possible is to call God a liar. We must take our spiritual
condition seriously.

Every believer is either cooperating with God or he is not; each
must learn to operate by faith *alone* in the promises of God to
the Church. The regenerated human spirit of every saint has been
washed clean by faith in the Gospel and made habitable for God
to dwell, but that does not mean Christians cannot entertain
unrighteous thoughts; we can and do. When a person aligns his

will with God's will, renews his mind with truth, and reckons himself dead to sin, he is free. Using God's boundless power, he is able to mature in his faith and bring glory to his Lord in all things.

As ye have therefore received Christ Jesus the Lord, so walk ye in him: (Col 2:6)

Now unto him that is able to do exceeding abundantly above all that we ask or think, according to the power that worketh in us... (Eph 3:20)

Thanks be unto God for his unspeakable gift. (2 Cor 9:15)

Chapter Six

Imputation, Baptism, and the New Covenant

KEY CONCEPTS:

- Imputation is the foundational doctrine of our position "in Christ." It means that God has credited to us what Jesus accomplished through His death, burial, and resurrection.
- Practical imputation, or "reckoning," is the means by which we access the benefits of our position in Christ. It is to count to be true those things which are true in the mind of God.
- The word "baptism" is best understood as "to identify with."
- One's will and testament does not go into effect until after one's death.

Every Christian has three enemies: the flesh, Satan, and Satan's world system. A Christian who does not operate as a spiritual man has little power against any of them. If he has not learned to count himself dead to the ungodly impulses, appetites, and attitudes of his own flesh, then neither does he have the spiritual maturity necessary to walk free from the influence of Satan and the world. Therefore, a Christian must first learn to live free from the dominion of his own flesh. The importance of Romans Chapter Six for Christian living cannot be overstated. It explains the mechanics of spiritual baptism, imputation, and freedom from sin through resurrection power. Having covered in detail the battle that exists within a Christian, we now turn to those truths which we are to know and use to set ourselves free from the swamp of the flesh.

Imputation

Romans Chapter Six contains much information about a body of doctrine called "positional truth," meaning those things which are true because of the believer's position "in Christ." The blessings of our position are things which have been imputed; they have already been accomplished by Christ, and are credited to the saints. In other words, God counts things to be true about Christians which are true about Jesus Christ. Since they are true in the mind of God, we must also count them to be true.

The doctrine of imputation is the "what" of our position in Christ. In Romans Chapter Six, that which is described as having been imputed to the believer is the death, burial, and resurrection of Jesus Christ. Because Jesus died on our behalf, it is as if each saint died with Him. Jesus was buried, and each of us is counted to have been buried with Him. We are also counted as resurrected with Him, able to access the power that raised Him from the grave. Spiritual baptism is the "how" of our position; it is the means by which the imputed benefits were applied to us. Spiritual baptism is a change in location that occurred in the mind of God; it is a transfer (Col 1:13). Our movement from being identified with

Adam to identified with Christ provided us with "every spiritual blessing in the heavenlies" (Eph 1:3).

Contrasting Spiritual Baptism with the Baptism of John

It is often helpful to explain something by explaining what it is not. The Bible describes many baptisms, and there is much confusion about the word "baptism," the meaning of which has nothing to do with water. Many people trust in water baptism for their standing before God, and some teach that the baptism in Romans Chapter Six is water baptism. Water, however, is not a picture of Christ's death. Jesus did not drown. He was not buried at sea. Water had nothing to do with the manner of His death, burial, or resurrection. The water baptisms performed by John did not picture Jesus' death either; the details of His death on a cross for sin were a secret and were not publicly displayed.

> *Which none of the princes of this world knew: for had they known it, they would not have crucified the Lord of glory.* (1 Cor 2:8)

Jesus was baptized in accordance with the law, in preparation for His ministry. It was a Jewish ceremonial ritual, a priestly cleansing (2 Chrn 4:6), and a sign to Israel (Jhn 1:31). Many Jews were baptized by John to identify with good news of the kingdom: the message that the prophesied earthly kingdom was at hand.

> *From that time Jesus began to preach, and to say, Repent: for the kingdom of heaven is at hand. … And Jesus went about all Galilee, teaching in their synagogues, and preaching the **gospel of the kingdom**, and healing all manner of sickness and all manner of disease among the people.* (Mat 4:17, 23; note: Jesus' miracles were kingdom signs, foreshadowing conditions in the millennial Kingdom of Heaven)

There are other differences as well when we compare John's baptism to spiritual baptism. When a Christian believes the Gospel of Christ, his spiritual birth renovates his human spirit (regeneration), but John's water baptism did not spiritually change those who practiced it. Those who identified with John's message still needed to be born again (Jhn 3:3-8).

Israel as a nation rejected Christ, but many Jewish individuals believed He was Messiah. When the secret of His payment for sin was revealed, those who trusted the Gospel of Christ for salvation were born again and became the first members of the Church. As Paul began his ministry, he found people who believed in the arrival of the Messiah, but had not heard the new revelation. In at least one case Paul re-baptized them, apparently to make it clear that they were identifying with the new message—the good news that Christ had died for sins. Paul, however, did not require water baptism and never taught that it had a role in salvation.

> *He said unto them, Have ye received the Holy Ghost since ye believed? And they said unto him, We have not so much as heard whether there be any Holy Ghost. And he said unto them, Unto what then were ye baptized? And they said, Unto John's baptism. Then said Paul, John verily baptized with the baptism of repentance, saying unto the people, that they should believe on him which should come after him, that is, on Christ Jesus. When they heard* this, *they were baptized in the name of the Lord Jesus.* (Act 19:2-5)

> *For Christ sent me not to baptize, but to preach the gospel…* (1 Cor 1:17a)

John's water baptism was a call to the Israelites to identify with *his* message—the good news that the earthly, millennial Kingdom of Heaven was at hand because the King had arrived. Blending Jesus' earthly, law-based ministry to the nation of Israel with his gracious, spiritual relationship with His body, the Church, leads to doctrinal error. The word "baptism" is found in both Jesus' ministry to Israel and in the grace doctrines to the Church, so how can we understand baptism according to grace?

One Lord, One Faith, One Baptism

"To identify with" is the best way to understand the word "baptism" in the epistles. A Christian's spiritual baptism does not identify him with Israel's earthly kingdom; rather, it is a spiritual transaction which permanently identifies each believer with Christ as the head of the Church, and specifically with His death, burial, and resurrection. The baptism in Romans Chapter Six (and also in Colossians Chapter Two) is referring to burial in a grave, not to Jewish ritual washings. The spiritual identification with Christ's death, burial, and resurrection is the "one baptism" referred to in Ephesians 4:5.

Because our imputed benefits come through Holy Spirit baptism—including the power to live free of the swamp of the flesh—understanding it is of great importance. Baptism is a spiritual "relocation" which took us from our position "in Adam" and placed us into a newly created spiritual entity known as the body of Christ, the Church. In the mind of God, the believer is now dead to everything he was "in Adam." It is as if each of us was placed in the grave with Jesus, died to everything we were, and then resurrected with Him. Through our identification with His resurrection, we are credited with spiritual power which enables us to live in accordance with our position in Christ and free from our spiritual enemies. We must know it and use it; there is no other way to live free.

The New Covenant: In His Blood

The Law and its ceremonies, such as ritual cleansings, were part of the Old Covenant which was in effect *before* Christ's death. After Israel's rejection of her Messiah, God instituted a new covenant, offered to all the people of the world. The new covenant (testament) is in His blood; like any will and testament, it went into effect *after* Christ's death.

> *Likewise also the cup after supper, saying, This cup is the new testament in my blood, which is shed for you.* (Lk 22:20; see also Mt 26:28, Mk 14:24, 1 Cor 11:25)

> *In whom we have redemption through his blood, the forgiveness of sins, according to the riches of his grace;* (Eph 1:7; see also Col 1:14)

> *For where a testament is, there must also of necessity be the death of the testator. For a testament is of force after men are dead: otherwise it is of no strength at all while the testator liveth.* (Heb 9:16-17)

The old covenant was for the nation of Israel. Those who share in the new covenant are the members of the Church, the body of Christ. The placement of the believer into this spiritual body is supernatural and invisible; it is not by the dipping of water baptism. Nor is water baptism a part of salvation, which was fully accomplished on the cross.

A person who believes the Gospel is immediately and permanently changed in two ways: he is made spiritually alive (regenerated), and he is permanently identified (spiritually baptized) with Christ. The indwelling of regeneration (Christ in me) and Holy Spirit baptism (me in Christ) are the two supernatural transactions that accompany initial faith. Both are 100% spiritual, and not in any way physical. A correct understanding of Holy Spirit baptism is necessary for a Christian to operate as a spiritual man, because he must count to be true (reckon) what God says is true and has credited to him (imputation). Romans Chapter Six details these truths, and will be further explained in the following two chapters of this book.

> ...even *God, who quickeneth the dead* (regeneration),
> *and calleth those things which be not as though they were*
> (imputation of spiritual baptism). (Ro 4:17b)

Romans 6:1-12

1 What shall we say then? Shall we continue in sin, that grace may abound? 2 God forbid. How shall we, that are dead to sin, live any longer therein? 3 Know ye not, that so many of us as were baptized into Jesus Christ were baptized into his death? 4 Therefore we are buried with him by baptism into death: that like as Christ was raised up from the dead by the glory of the Father, even so we also should walk in newness of life. 5 For if we have been planted together in the likeness of his death, we shall be also in the likeness of his *resurrection: 6 Knowing this, that our old man is crucified with* him, *that the body of sin might be destroyed, that henceforth we should not serve sin. 7 For he that is dead is freed from sin. 8 Now if we be dead with Christ, we believe that we shall also live with him: 9 Knowing that Christ being raised from the dead dieth no more; death hath no more dominion over him. 10 For in that he died, he died unto sin once: but in that he liveth, he liveth unto God. 11 Likewise reckon ye also yourselves to be dead indeed unto sin, but alive unto God through Jesus Christ our Lord. 12 Let not sin therefore reign in your mortal body, that ye should obey it in the lusts thereof.*

Chapter Seven

Reckoning in Practice:
Romans 6:1-12

KEY CONCEPTS:

- To reckon is to count true something that has already been completed.
- The power of God's grace is for the purpose of living free from sin.
- The law of sin is not dead; we are to count ourselves dead to it.
- Grace does not require circumstances to change for it to be effective.

Romans Chapter Six is Paul's detailed explanation of the basis of our freedom from the flesh and exactly how to use it. He begins with a reminder that Christ's payment for sin is not for the purpose of sinning more; it is just the opposite. Christians have been released from the jail cell of the flesh and should have no desire to return to it. In order to remain free, we must count (reckon) those things to be true which God has counted to be true of us. In other words, He has imputed them to us; reckon and impute refer to the same doctrine.

Reckoning Compared to Faith

Reckoning is an important term for Christian living, especially in regard to the way in which it is different than faith. Faith knows that the promises of God for tomorrow are coming, and faith makes actual His promises for today.

> *Now faith is the substance of things hoped for...* (Heb 11:1a; something promised is expected and substantiated by faith.)

For example, the saint who believes that he has the ability to be content in any situation will experience contentment. This promise has been *imparted*, meaning it has literally been given to the members of Christ's body and can be experienced, in the present, by faith. This is what spirituality is; it is what we have because we are regenerated—**Christ in me.** Any saint can emanate the character of the indwelling Spirit; he can experience and express kindness, love, joy, peace, self-control, patience, boldness, courage, freedom from cares and anxieties, and much more—all by faith— because God says He has provided those real, experiential things.

Here is how reckoning is different: One who reckons himself dead with Christ did not literally die on the cross. He did not and does not experience burial or crucifixion. Things which are to be reckoned by us have been *imputed* by God, meaning they are counted to be so. This is positional truth; it is what we have through our spiritual baptism into Christ—**me in Christ.** To reckon is to believe in something that has already been accomplished by Christ; it is to count a promise to be true which is not actual in one's present experience. Therefore, even though the law of sin is not dead—it remains operational within the human body—the Christian who reckons himself dead to it need not obey it. He may feel it, but he need not act. God says he is free, so he is free.

Don't You Know About Imputation? Romans 6:1-4

Every believer has been freed from the dominion of sin, no matter how much sin he has committed. In Romans 5:20, Paul explained that grace is *super-abundant* in comparison to the abundance of sin, adding in 6:1-2 that this fact is surely not a reason to sin. God's grace has freed us so that we might not sin; any Christian who understands and appreciates God's purpose in grace would not endeavor to return to sin's bondage and dishonor Christ's sacrifice. Those who have enjoyed the glorious liberty of the sons of God find no appeal in returning to the mire.

> *What shall we say then? Shall we continue in sin, that grace may abound? God forbid. How shall we, that are dead to sin, live any longer therein?* (Ro 6:1-2)

Christian freedom from the law of sin is described as being "dead to sin." It is accomplished by applying the doctrine of imputation: We are to count to be true and use those things which have been credited to us through our spiritual baptism.

> *Know ye not, that so many of us as were baptized into Jesus Christ were baptized into his death? Therefore we are buried with him by baptism into death: that like as Christ was raised up from the dead by the glory of the Father, even so we also should walk in newness of life.* (Ro 6:3-4)

Those things which Jesus accomplished on the cross are credited to each one who believes the Gospel of Christ, 1 Corinthians 15:1-4. In the mind of God, it is as if that person was on the cross with Jesus, justly punished for his own sins. This is so because Jesus was the substitutionary sacrifice for all mankind. He took upon Himself sin, giving Himself as a sacrifice for the sins of the world.

God the Father poured out His wrath upon the infinite person, God the Son, against an infinite number of sins. That spiritual transaction on the cross paid the debt owed to God for every sin. Each one who believes the Gospel is credited with Jesus' payment, immediately receiving all its benefits. The payment for sin having been satisfied frees us to walk in a new quality of life.

> *For the love of Christ compels us, because we judge thus: that if One died for all, then all died;* (2 Cor 5:14 NKJV)

Dead *and* Buried: Romans 6:5-8

> *For if we have been planted together* in the likeness *of* his *death, we shall be also in the likeness of his resurrection: Knowing this, that our old man* (our position in Adam) *is crucified with* him*, that the body of sin might be destroyed* (deprived of influence)*, that henceforth we should not serve sin.* (Ro 6:5-6; clarification added: Adam is the old man, Christ is the new man.)

Just as the Christian is counted to have died on that cross, he is counted as buried with Christ as well. In this tender picture of the source of Christian maturity, burial is pictured as planting two seeds in the same hole, becoming two plants entwined, growing up together from the place they were planted. The believer's close identification with Christ's death *and burial* enables him to count himself dead and buried in regard to sin so that he can live in resurrection power rather than under the dominion of sin. Burial should not be discounted. Counting himself dead and buried, the spiritual man then grows up together with Christ, unto Christlikeness.

Wherefore laying aside (in the grave) *all malice, and all guile, and hypocrisies, and envies, and all evil speakings,* (1 Pet 2:1)

In the mind of God, we are dead to everything we were in Adam. A person who died and is buried is not tempted to sin:

For he that is dead is freed from sin. (Ro 6:7)

Our Christian life is to reflect positional truth in daily living; we are to know our position, use its power, identify with Christ—even in suffering—and reckon ourselves dead to sin. Circumstances, history, feelings, experiences, and the desires of the swamp are irrelevant.

That I may know him, and the power of his resurrection, and the fellowship of his sufferings, being made conformable unto his death; (Phil 3:10)

Resurrected: Romans 6:8-13

Now if we be dead with Christ, we believe that we shall also live with him… (Ro 6:8)

He who has believed the Gospel of Christ is free from death: it does not reign over him. Paul explained in Romans 5:14, 17, and 21 that death reigned over mankind as a king, but those who have God's grace reign over death! Neither sin nor death has power over those who are already counted as dead and buried. Furthermore, Christ's work on our behalf was accomplished *once*, a sufficient sacrifice for the sins of the world. It will never be repeated. Every Christian is credited with Jesus' work and is sufficiently equipped to live according to God's will, as revealed in scripture.

Knowing that Christ being raised from the dead dieth no more; death hath no more dominion over him. For in that he died, he died unto sin once: but in that he liveth, he liveth unto God. (Ro 6:9-10)

The power displayed in the resurrection is the same power that enables the new life in Christ. The Christian, therefore, is called to reckon to be true what God says is true: We have been purchased out of the slave market of the law of sin, and need not live in bondage to sin of any kind. Every Christian is equipped to live an obedient, holy, fruitful, victorious Christian life.

Likewise reckon ye also yourselves to be dead indeed unto sin, but alive unto God through Jesus Christ our Lord. (Ro 6:11)

Let not sin therefore reign in your mortal body, that ye should obey it in the lusts thereof. (Ro 6:12)

You Can't Tempt Me; I'm Dead!

That sin is a choice is made clear by Paul's exhortation to deny sin. It is important to remember this distinction: Sin is not dead; the Christian is dead to it. To be dead to sins is to react to temptation as would a dead man. The temptation exists, but a dead (mortified) body does not respond to it.

*Who his own self bare our sins in his own body on the tree, that we, **being dead to sins**, should live unto righteousness: by whose stripes ye were healed* (from those sins). (1 Pet 2:24; clarification added)

Using this mindset, the spiritual man does not allow himself to be led into sin, but instead determines to align himself with God. He then uses his spiritual tools in order that his body be used as an instrument of righteousness for the glory of God. He does not remain as a dead man; he is as a dead man *only in regard to sin*, but he is alive and useful for God.

I beseech you therefore, brethren, by the mercies of God, that ye present your bodies a living sacrifice, holy, acceptable unto God, which is *your reasonable service.* (Ro 12:1)

Always bearing about in the body the dying of the Lord Jesus, that the life also of Jesus might be made manifest in our body. (2 Cor 4:10)

… For if ye live after the flesh, ye shall die: but if ye through the Spirit do mortify the deeds of the body, ye shall live (Ro 8:13)

But I keep under my body, and bring it *into subjection: lest that by any means, when I have preached to others, I myself should be a castaway* (from usefulness, from service). (1 Cor 9:27; clarification added)

God says that Christians are counted as having died on the cross with Christ and buried with Him. When we experience temptation from the swamp of the flesh, we are to reckon this to be true. To reckon is to count sufficient something which has already been accomplished. It might look like this: "I have been made free. I do not have to do this. It doesn't matter how it feels. God says this is true and it is. I have the power that raised Christ from the grave to keep me from sin." When we count to be true what God says is true, we access the resurrection power of God's grace. This power enables us to operate free from sin, and, thereby, live in accordance with our exalted position in Christ. If a saint thinks otherwise— that he cannot withstand temptation to sin, for example—he is either deceived or lacking understanding of his new position in Christ. It may take many mental reviews of this doctrine before a Christian truly comprehends that he is free. For the Christian who keeps rereading Romans Chapter Six, his mind will become convinced and freedom will come.

> *Jesus answered them, Verily, verily, I say unto you, Whosoever committeth sin is the servant of sin. … If the Son therefore shall make you free, ye shall be free indeed.* (Jhn 8:34, 36)

Romans 6:13-23

13 Neither yield ye your members as instruments of unrighteousness unto sin: but yield yourselves unto God, as those that are alive from the dead, and your members as instruments of righteousness unto God. 14 For sin shall not have dominion over you: for ye are not under the law, but under grace. 15 What then? shall we sin, because we are not under the law, but under grace? God forbid. 16 Know ye not, that to whom ye yield yourselves servants to obey, his servants ye are to whom ye obey; whether of sin unto death, or of obedience unto righteousness? 17 But God be thanked, that ye were the servants of sin, but ye have obeyed from the heart that form of doctrine which was delivered you. 18 Being then made free from sin, ye became the servants of righteousness. 19 I speak after the manner of men because of the infirmity of your flesh: for as ye have yielded your members servants to uncleanness and to iniquity unto iniquity; even so now yield your members servants to righteousness unto holiness. 20 For when ye were the servants of sin, ye were free from righteousness. 21 What fruit had ye then in those things whereof ye are now ashamed? for the end of those things is death. 22 But now being made free from sin, and become servants to God, ye have your fruit unto holiness, and the end everlasting life. 23 For the wages of sin is death; but the gift of God is eternal life through Jesus Christ our Lord.

Chapter Eight
Know, Reckon, Yield:
Romans 6:13-23

KEY CONCEPTS:

- The definition of eternal life is to know God.
- Eternal life is a quality of life that is available right now.
- Things imputed to us have already been accomplished by Christ.
- We access imputed benefits by reckoning: by counting to be true what God says is true.

Romans Chapter Six continues Paul's teaching of imputation, explaining its practical application with three words: know, reckon, and yield. Understanding imputation is necessary to utilize the benefits of this doctrine: the fact that those things which are imputed are *already accomplished* is the key aspect of this foundational truth. We appropriate our imputed benefits by knowing and understanding them, counting them as already having been accomplished, and yielding to resurrection power rather than to the law of sin in the flesh.

Know

And this is life eternal, that they might know thee the only
true God, and Jesus Christ, whom thou hast sent. (Jhn 17:3)

In John's Gospel we find the definition of eternal life: it is to know
God. Knowing is the core of the grace-through-faith program,
because faith requires an object: we must know something in
order to believe in it. Furthermore, Christians do not have a hide-
and-seek relationship with our Father; we can rest assured that
God has written, preserved, and promised to teach us what He
wants and expects us to know (Jhn 14:26, 1 Pet 1:25). Several times
throughout Romans Chapter Six, Paul calls us to "know."

Reviewing What We Need to Know

To walk free from sin, a Christian must know that he can. When
facing temptation, he must remember that he always has a choice—
to cooperate with the law of sin in his members (carnality) or
with the law of God after the inward man (spirituality). Every
human being in every moment serves either God or sin; there is no
"neutral," nor any combination of part sin and part righteousness.
When temptation arises, a saint can reckon himself free and
continue as a spiritual man, or he can succumb and serve his
flesh. The Bible is absolutely clear that there are only two options,
and a Christian must know this in order to discern which system
he is using.

As Paul explained in the opening verses of Romans Chapter Six,
the Christian is dead in regard to sin and temptation. In the mind
of God, each saint died with Jesus and was in the grave, buried with
Jesus. Therefore, a Christian has the ability to respond to it as if he
is a dead man—unmoved by temptation.

God identifies the Christian with Jesus' death, burial, and resurrection, and He calls this baptism. It is a purely spiritual, one-time, one-way transaction that occurred at the moment of faith in the Gospel of Christ. But we were not left in the grave. In the mind of God, the Christian has also been resurrected with Jesus and has been given access to a new power for living, called resurrection life. Resurrection life did not replace or eradicate our human nature, which remains sinful. It is a new option that enables us to live differently than any saint since the fall of mankind: in newness of life.

To "walk in newness of life" is the furthest thing from continuing in sin. In imputation *we* are counted as having died on that cross; therefore, we can count ourselves dead to the law of sin. The law of sin is not dead; we are dead to it. In the Christians' new position in Christ, we are no longer located in Adam, in the slave market of sin, but seated in the heavenlies with Him. It is as if we were placed into a new office because that is where we will work in our new job.

> *And hath raised* us *up together, and made* us *sit together in heavenly* places *in Christ Jesus:* (Eph 2:6)

> *If ye then be risen with Christ, seek those things which are above, where Christ sitteth on the right hand of God.* (Col 3:1)

To "know" is a vitally important part of spiritual freedom. No one can serve God without knowing God's will as written in God's word. Knowing who we are in Christ, what we have, and how to access the power of God's grace is the first step toward freedom from the swamp of the flesh.

Reckoning our New Position

Spiritual baptism is a transfer; it is a transaction in which the believer is moved from his position "in Adam" to his new position "in Christ." In the mind of God, the Christian is forever identified with Christ and will never again be identified with Adam. Because the sin principle still lives, however, the believer always has the choice to continue to *serve* sin. Salvation in practice is for the purpose of living free from sin, "that the body of sin might be destroyed," meaning to be made inactive, to deprive of influence, and to render inoperative. Colossians Chapter Two provides another description of our identification with Christ, our head, and the freedom it provides.

> *And ye are complete in him, which is the head of all principality and power: In whom also ye are circumcised with the circumcision made without hands,* (definition of spiritual circumcision:) *in putting off the body of the sins of the flesh by the circumcision of Christ:* **Buried with** him **in baptism**, *wherein also ye are risen with him through the faith of the operation of God, who hath raised him from the dead. And you, being dead in your sins and the uncircumcision of your flesh, hath he* (now) *quickened together* (made spiritually alive in regeneration) *with him, having forgiven you all trespasses; Blotting out the handwriting of ordinances* (the defunct law system given to the Jews) *that was against us, which was contrary to us, and took it out of the way, nailing it to his cross;* (Col 2:10-14; clarification added)

The believer who is tempted might say to himself, "I know I am free not to sin. I know that Jesus already accomplished everything needed to make me free. God sees me as free. I must count it to be true, as He does. I do not need to yield to this temptation. I yield myself to God for his righteous purpose." Regularly renewing the mind with these truths increases our reliance and trust in God's declaration of our freedom from sin. This is maturity.

Yield to Grace: Romans 6:13

Neither yield ye your members as *instruments of unrighteousness unto sin: but yield yourselves unto God, as those that are alive from the dead, and your members* as *instruments of righteousness unto God.* (Ro 6:13)

To yield is to take God's side in a matter, literally to "stand beside." The Christian who yields himself has chosen spirituality over carnality. He has deprived the law of sin from using the members (parts) of his body. His physical members are now useful tools for God. It cannot be stated strongly enough that if a Christian is not operating as a spiritual man, it does not matter that he is doing what he thinks is a "good work." Even that is tainted by sin by the very use of his unrighteous hands, feet, or mouth to do it. Works tainted by sin are not acceptable to God. Christian living is much less about what we do, and is always about our spiritual condition in whatever we are doing. One's condition must change from carnal to spiritual by accessing the power of God's grace to operate by the law of God after the inward man (Ro 7:22). If a Christian has ceased the sin in question, and confesses agreement with God in regard to it, he returns to operating by faith as a spiritual man. If he yet needs to stop sinning, he must reckon himself free from it, allowing positional truth to convince his mind that he has been made free.

Yielding is not Law: Romans 6:14

Know, reckon, and yield are the elements of an internal, spiritual transaction that happens when a Christian desires to honor Christ's sacrifice to save him from temptation to sin in daily living. The Christian who uses this spiritual power is not under nor obligated to any kind of law for his Christian walk, but is operating by the grace system. He does not say, "I am not allowed to do this." He says instead, "I am free from succumbing to this temptation."

> *For sin shall not have dominion over you: for ye are not under the law, but under grace.* (Ro 6:14)

Operating by using law gives the principle of sin dominion over the person who uses it. The saint who uses personal willpower or external limits to control behavior has abandoned the law of God after the inward man which provides victory. We cannot use the faith system and a flesh system at the same time. To yield is to appropriate the power of God's grace and trust it to enable godly obedience. We are taking God's side rather than siding with our flesh in whatever way it is trying to influence us—a physical craving, a poor attitude, or an ungodly thought. We yield to righteousness because we want to obey God; we are convinced that His way is better than anything.

Grace is Never for Licentiousness: Romans 6:15-16

> *As free, and not using your liberty for a cloke of maliciousness, but as the servants of God.* (1 Pet 2:16; see also Gal 5:13)

Freedom from law is certainly not lawlessness; it does not mean that the Christian need not obey earthly laws. It means that he obeys laws by the power of God's grace. He might say to himself,

"I am tempted to break this law, and I don't agree with it, but God has empowered me to be free from my rebellious impulse and submit to earthly authorities." The spiritual man is willing to cooperate with the authorities (assuming they are acting legally) with a good attitude, not begrudgingly, because his intention is to glorify God. The internal power of God's grace is his motivation; he is not showing mere external submission. Grace works an internal change that often has external results as well (Eph 6:6, Col 3:22).

God has a gracious, forgiving attitude toward His children because His justice was met on the cross. The complete satisfaction of mankind's sin debt makes the Christian who has accepted it clean from sin in the eyes of God. This allows God to indwell and empower the spiritual man to do His will. God's grace is not for licentiousness; it does not free a Christian to sin, but instead frees him *not to sin*.

> *What then? shall we sin, because we are not under the law, but under grace? God forbid. Know ye not, that to whom ye yield yourselves servants to obey, his servants ye are to whom ye obey; whether of sin unto death, or of obedience unto righteousness?* (Ro 6:15-16)

The implications of a Christian returning to the sinfulness from which he has been freed are many, ranging from earthly consequences to physical death (1 Cor 3:15, 11:30; Heb 12:5-11). Yielding to the law of sin always leads to spiritual death (Ro 7:11), meaning separation from fellowship with God. Obeying the law of God after the inward man enables a God-honoring life that is of an acceptable quality.

You Will Yield to Something: Romans 6:17-23

In biblical usage, the heart of man is the seat of decision-making. The heart is associated with love, because when we love someone, we choose to be with them and do things for them—to help, benefit, and delight them. As a picture of an internal operation, the heart reflects a person's affections, desires, and priorities through the choices that he makes, whether good or bad.

> *...They do alway err in* their *heart; and they have not known my ways.* (Heb 3:10b; note that error results from a lack of knowledge.)

It is man's choice to reject or to obey God, including the call of the Gospel to believe it. Every Christian was a slave to sin until he obeyed the Gospel by accepting that message as the true word of God unto salvation. The purpose of deliverance from the slave market of sin is to devote oneself to the glory of the Deliverer. Paul refers to this as becoming a servant of righteousness.

> *But God be thanked, that ye were the servants of sin, but ye have obeyed **from the heart** that form of doctrine which was delivered you. Being then made free from sin, ye became the servants of righteousness.* (Ro 6:17-18)

The Christian's devotion to God is not out of obligation, but out of love and the conviction that it is worthwhile and beneficial. A spiritual man is convinced that God's way is best. His gratitude for his deliverance from hellfire and from the slavery of sinfulness leads him to boast of God's mercy, love, and power. He shares the Gospel of Christ, speaks of God's character, and teaches His word to others. In this way he is a servant unto holiness. His life is set apart for God's use and glory, in accordance with God's will, which is plainly conveyed in the letters to the Church.

> *I speak after the manner of men because of the infirmity of your flesh: for as ye have yielded your members servants to uncleanness and to iniquity unto iniquity; even so now yield your members servants to righteousness unto holiness.* (Ro 6:19)

Paul reminds his readers that sinfulness is progressive; iniquity is unto further iniquity. The believer is called to yield himself to God in order to avoid living lawlessly, meaning to live without using the law of God after the inward man. Christians absolutely do sin and must continually choose to answer the call to live rightly, as defined by God's instructions to the Church.

For the natural man, operating in the flesh is the only option; he is "free from righteousness" according to God. This does not mean that an unsaved person cannot do a good deed, but even his most righteous acts do not qualify him for a life in God's presence (Is 64:6). They are not of a righteous quality and are, therefore, not acceptable to God.

> *For when ye were the servants of sin, ye were **free from righteousness**. What fruit had ye then in those things whereof ye are now ashamed? for the end of those things is death.* (Ro 6:20-21)

Before the cross, nobody was free from sin. "But now," we are under a new administration. The cross work of Christ has provided deliverance from the bondage of sin, opening the door to an eternal quality of life, every day and forever.

*But **now** being made free from sin, and become servants*
to God, ye have your fruit unto holiness, and the end (aim,
purpose) *everlasting* (eternal) *life. For the **wages** of sin is*
*death; but the **gift** of God is eternal life through* (in) *Jesus*
Christ our Lord. (Ro 6:22-23, clarification and literal words
added; notice that "in" refers to our position in Christ.)

Knowing one's identity in Christ, reckoning it to be true, and
yielding to God are the elements that deliver the Christian from
the power of sin. The spiritual man enjoys the eternal quality of life
that is enjoyed by the members of the Godhead. He is filled with
peace, joy, love, and many other wonderful things, because he has
been made free from his sin-cursed flesh. Rather than earning
the wages of sin which separate him from fellowship with God,
he rests in the gracious gift of deliverance from sin. The doctrines
of grace are the "present truth" which set us free and keep us free
from the law of sin.

Wherefore I will not be negligent to put you always in
remembrance of these things, though ye know them, and
be established in the present truth. (2 Pet 1:12)

Conclusion

He Did it All

Good Gifts

God's children are the heirs to His kingdom, and are intended to receive an inheritance. Because this life is a training ground for the next one, those who do not cooperate with God will not be prepared to rule and reign with Him in His kingdom. Therefore, practicing sin adversely affects the inheritance of the child of God, but it does not change the fact that he has been born into God's family. We will protect and treasure our inheritance if our conviction is that what we have been promised is infinitely valuable and better than anything.

A Sufficient Provision

Verses that describe a loss of reward are sometimes misunderstood as if salvation can be somehow undone. The Lord of Glory is not a fool who suffered the wrath of God upon the cross to provide a gift that is temporary, ineffective, or only partially functional. Neither did He die in order to try to get us to do something else to be saved from the penalty of sin. He did it all. He also made us free. The freedom Christ's sacrifice provided from the power of sin works perfectly and works every time—if we use it. We who desire to be Spirit-filled must learn to recognize temptation and the desires and impulses within our own swamp. Then we must know what Christ provided, reckon it to be true, and yield ourselves to His righteousness. Know, reckon, and yield begin with choosing to obey God because He is good, all His intentions are good, and His provisions are sufficient for all our needs.

Faith for Big Things and Small

In our own Christian lives, we, the authors, received much instruction over several years before we truly grasped and instituted daily operation by the power of grace. It didn't seem necessary to walk by faith when doing the dishes or raking the yard. But a Christian can do household chores with a downcast attitude, grudgingly, or with a blank mind; this is a default to the flesh. The desires, attitudes, and priorities of the Christian are transformed whenever he is Spirit-filled. It is not automatic; it is the result of knowing and intentionally directing faith toward the promises of God to the Church. Even the most mundane activities which result from spirituality bring glory to God and eternal reward to the saint. It changes their *quality*, making those things good and acceptable in the sight of God.

In both Romans and Corinthians, Paul mentions exercising faith even in eating food, one of the most common, ordinary things that we do. The issue was whether he was taking God into account even in that small thing. The meal in question was a potential stumbling block to another believer; therefore, the motive for and the wisdom of eating it was a spiritual matter. Similarly, the purpose of praying at mealtime is to get rightly adjusted to God so to eat by faith, with a correct, God-honoring mindset. Mature Christian living includes God in the mundane, not just the "big things" in life. By grasping the concept of using the correct method of operation, a Christian can move on to maturity, maintaining his spiritual condition in whatever he faces in daily living. Doing so brings meaning and value to even the smallest tasks.

Living Free

But whoso looketh into the perfect law of liberty, and
continueth therein, *he being not a forgetful hearer, but*
a doer of the work, this man shall be blessed in his deed.
(Ja 1:25)

God asks many things of us. In another sense, He only asks us to know Him and believe what He says in His word. If we do so, the other things will follow. If we believe that what God offers is better than anything, including Him in every part of life is more than worth the effort to learn His word. Everything He asks is good because He is always and only good. He is a blessing and benefit to all who desire to know Him, and He benefits everything in which He is included.

If the topic of this book is new to you, read Romans Chapter Six every day for a month. Then read it weekly for several weeks. Then add Chapter Seven. We, the authors, believe that victory over the flesh is so vital, that every Christian should read these chapters monthly for the rest of their lives. We have been studying, reading, and rereading them for many years in order to quickly recognize the operation of the flesh and incorporate the method of victory into daily living. It is still difficult at times, hence the need to continually renew the mind with spiritual truth (Ro 12:2, Eph 4:23).

We are all bombarded with ungodly messages and influences every single day. Our flesh never relents, nor does our adversary—the prince of the power of the air and the god of this age. No Christian can defeat the adversary without learning to walk free from the swamp within. Understanding Romans Chapters Six and Seven is essential for a victorious Christian life which glorifies God and provides peace, joy, and contentment to the believer. No Christian can do so without the meat of the word.

God does not deny that one can be sinning and having fun at the same time. Whether it is the cathartic feeling of telling someone exactly what you think, or that scrumptious second helping at dinner, the swamp can be enjoyable for a while (Heb 11:25). God gave us bodies that can experience many pleasant things and souls that can feel joy and delight, and we can enjoy them rightly when we are spiritual. God is not a meanie who wants to rob us of things we like. He is simply trying to convince us that whether it is in the moment or for a lifetime, the reward of operating according to holiness is much, much better than anything our sinful nature craves. Furthermore, the enjoyment of the flesh and the world is fleeting and sometimes has negative consequences. What God offers is eternal reward. If we trust in Him, the struggles of today will prepare us for an unspeakably wonderful future. God is always good.

> But exhort one another daily, while it is called To day; lest any of you be hardened through the deceitfulness of sin. (Heb 3:13)

> Charge them that are rich in this world, that they be not highminded, nor trust in uncertain riches, but in the living God, who giveth us richly all things to enjoy; (1 Tim 6:17)

I counsel thee to buy of me gold tried in the fire, that thou mayest be rich; and white raiment, that thou mayest be clothed, and that *the shame of thy nakedness do not appear; and anoint thine eyes with eyesalve, that thou mayest see.* (Rev 3:18)

For ye had compassion of me in my bonds, and took joyfully the spoiling of your goods, knowing in yourselves that ye have in heaven a better and an enduring substance. (Heb 10:34)

16 *But now they desire a better* country, *that is, an heavenly: wherefore God is not ashamed to be called their God: for he hath prepared for them a city.* (Heb 11:16)

About the Authors

Preston Condra and his wife Kelly serve in independent, full-time Christian ministry. Preston graduated from Oklahoma Baptist University and Southwestern Baptist Theological Seminary. His lifelong service has included preaching across the country, teaching, lecturing, writing, and appearing on broadcasts. Kelly has been speaking and teaching throughout her career. The Condras share a passion for the Gospel of Christ, found in 1 Corinthians 15:1–4. Through their ministry, *Sufficient Word*, they teach, preach, and offer training in evangelism and discipleship. They have co-authored and published many books, producing practical materials to help Christians share their faith and grow in grace. Through *By the Book Design and Book Management,* a consulting service, they help authors to professionally publish their books: *www.bythebook.design.*

sufficien✝word
MINISTRIES

www.sufficientword.com